Life

THE GREAT EDUCATOR

Life
THE GREAT EDUCATOR

DICKY McCUEN

COURIER PUBLISHING

Life, the Great Educator

ISBN 978-1-955295-17-8 (softcover)
ISBN 978-1-955295-18-5 (e-book)

Courier Publishing
100 Manly Street
Greenville, South Carolina 29601
CourierPublishing.com

PUBLISHED IN THE UNITED STATES OF AMERICA

DEDICATION

To Jesus Christ, to whom I owe everything;

to my wonderful wife, Rhonda,
for the never-ending love and support she gave me;

to Caroline, my daughter, a beautiful and talented educator;

to Jay, my son, a fireman, of whom I am immensely proud;

and to Johnathan, Annaliese, Fallon and Ellison,
the most wonderful grandchildren anyone could have.

Table of Contents

Preface

Life is a journey. Reading about the exploration of America, the oceans, the world, and space has always fueled my imagination. All these ventures have been a wonderful and exciting journey for the people who set out to explore and record their experiences for generations to enjoy and study.

I still remember watching as our astronauts landed on the moon. I believe every eye was fastened to the television, watching those heroes as they stepped out onto the lunar surface, putting up the United States flag and striking a golf ball.

These are just a sampling of the experiences that form a life to remember. Each of us should strive to leave a legacy behind that will be remembered — not just as a date on a tombstone, but a life that impacts the world around you. "A good and honest life is a blessed memorial" (Proverbs 10:7, MSG).

You don't have to be a great explorer or an astronaut to be remembered. You just need to be a caring and loving person to those around you. Do what is right and be forthright in all your interactions with the people you meet every day. Help someone along the way, even if it means deviating off your beaten path.

I know a man who lived in a small town on the side of a rocky hillside. The home he lived in had dirt for a floor and straw and mud for a roof. He was a lowly carpenter, but He changed the world. His life will never be forgotten! His name is Jesus. Yes, I realize He was God, but at the time He was also a man, a man who walked everywhere He traveled. His love for people is the reason His life is remembered to this day. If you want to leave a legacy to be remembered, then love people just as

He did. Love them so much that they know without a doubt you will give all you have in life, and your energy, to help them.

When you learn the world does not revolve around you, then you will learn to love as Jesus loved and live as Jesus lived.

I hope the words throughout the chapters of this book will be inspiring and helpful and, in some cases, a warning to help someone evade the wrong paths along life's journey.

"Enter through the narrow gate. For wide is the gate and broad is the road that leads to destruction, and many enter through it. But small is the gate and narrow the road that leads to life, and only a few find it" (Matthew 7:13-14, NIV).

Life

THE GREAT EDUCATOR

CHAPTER 1

CHERISH EVERY DAY

It is no secret that we are just passing through this world, and time is short, to say the least. God prompted James to write in James 4:14, "For what is your life? It is even a vapor that appears for a little time and then vanishes away." We would like to remove from our minds the fact that life has a termination date. The Bible tells us in Hebrews 9:27, "And as it is appointed for men to die once, but after this the judgment." Christians and non-Christians alike should keep the brevity of life in mind. You should not dwell on it; just know your time is limited.

I graduated in 1968 from Woodmont High School in Piedmont, South Carolina, at the age of seventeen. It seems that walking across the gym to receive my diploma on that wonderful spring night happened just yesterday, and now the sweet age of seventy has crept up on my driver's license. I can't believe over fifty years have landed in the history books. The years disappeared like steam off a hot pot of green beans. Where did the time go?

I made a major mistake with both my son Jay and my daughter Caroline when they were born. I blinked! Now they are married, and I have three beautiful grandchildren and one great-grandchild.

My wife and I attended my fiftieth class reunion on a beautiful Saturday afternoon at one of the wonderful churches in our community. When I walked through the door, I was fortunate to see one of my best friends from high school (and who still is to this day). Not only are we friends, our sons are too. When I walked into the room, which was nostalgic, with memorabilia from our school days displayed, I said to Doug, "These people look old, don't you think?" He smiled from ear to ear, just like the big bump on the log did fifty years ago.

We had a wonderful time talking about the good ole days. They were carefree days filled with laughter, joking and having fun — and a little bit of studying thrown in when the occasion called for it. We would go to the football games on Friday nights, and I remember how cold it would be, but you did not dare let anyone know you were cold because we were men — and men didn't get cold, no matter what. After the game, and on Saturday nights, we would cruise Main Street in my lustrous and charming black-on-black 1947 Chevy coupe, looking for girls, just having a good, clean time. It seems as if it were yesterday.

This experience is an illustration of how hurriedly years can pass by unnoticed. Most of you reading these words know exactly what I am saying. We are running against the clock. We have to be here by this time, there by that time. It never stops speeding along, seven days a week, as we do our best to get all the things we think are important completed by specific deadlines someone else set for us.

Proverbs 21:5 says, "The plans of the diligent lead surely to plenty, but those of everyone who is hasty, surely to poverty." I have found the faster someone does something, the more errors they make. There have been many important projects redone because of haste.

Life is not like playing golf with your friends on Saturday; a do-over or a mulligan is not an option. Some mistakes last a lifetime. We need to be conscientious with the things we do and never let time be the rule and guide of our life. Folks need to stop, take a break and smell the roses. People generally need to move over to the slow lane and take their time. You will see things you have been missing for years.

You may find a stress-free road off the beaten path, where you can drive slowly without horns blowing and cars riding your bumper by stressed-out folks in a hurry to get somewhere so they can scurry to the next place. The road you discover may be filled with beautiful trees and wildflowers adorned in many colors blooming along the roadside. If you look closely, you might see some extraordinary wildlife. Maybe even a farm with green pastures and rolling hills and, yes, even some cows or horses. A little further down the road you see the antebellum farmhouse with giant white columns reaching to the second floor with an early American light hanging from a chain. You can't help but notice the expansive porch with white rocking chairs perfectly decorated for the season. Standing in the front of the house between two giant oak trees flies Old Glory, waving freely in the breeze.

Letting your imagination take you away for a moment, you will see people on the porch passing the time of day, maybe swatting away a persistent fly or mosquito. The man is wearing bib overalls and well-worn work boots, dusty from plowing in the fields. Hanging out of the left side of his mouth is an old corncob pipe, the smell of apple in the smoke rising from the bowl. He is reading the newspaper, or maybe the Farmer's Almanac, checking out the best time to plant the next crop, or maybe looking for a decent price on a new bull for his herd. His beautiful wife, with her golden hair braided, is sewing a quilt she is making for the coming winter. Between them lies an old dog, snoring and enjoying life in the cool of the day. That ole dog has never won best in show, but he has won the hearts of the two people he lies between.

Should that not be enough, as you pass the house you see a magnificent two-story barn painted an eye-catching bright red with white trim, with the sun casting the shadows of the trees that grace the appearance of the backyard. The top floor is where the hay is stored for the cows you saw just back up the road. Hay can be seen hanging out the door, with a couple of cardinals picking seeds out of it. Below, there is a big green-and-yellow John Deere tractor with farm equipment attached, and an old black-and-white farm cat lying on the warm hood. And if you look closely, you will see a black-and-tan beagle stretched out in the shade under the tractor. Drive slowly, or you will miss the blessings that are right before your eyes. The detour will be a memory for you and your family for years to come.

I had always wanted to learn to fly. I thought it would be the most interesting adventure. One day Rhonda and I were riding near the airport, and there was a sign that said, "Learn to fly here." I turned in, and Rhonda said, "Surely you are not going to try to fly?" Yes, that was my intention. And fly, I did!

It was one of the most enjoyable adventures I have ever experienced. Flying gives you a feeling of freedom as you glide through the air high above the earth below. Flying on a commercial aircraft is not like piloting or being a passenger in a small plane. It is so exhilarating (not to mention, how much fun it is).

Rhonda and I would fly to Hilton Head Island and other destinations across our great state. It was so nice to arrive in less than half the time it would take to drive.

Rhonda was a little apprehensive about flying. She had a fear of the clouds, which she called puffs, and, of course, the possibility of dangerous weather. One beautiful summer day we decided to go to the beach in Charleston. As we were flying along, looking at the beauty below, I noticed a gigantic cloud between us and our destination. I made the decision to fly around the cloud when, all of a sudden, we were engulfed by the force of the storm. Rhonda went into panic mode. She was trying to get out of her seat to get to the back seat. She was making such a commotion, I had to push the microphone on her headset away from her mouth so I could pilot the plane out of the weather. I saw a small hole in the clouds about five hundred feet below and pointed the nose of the plane directly at the hole with full power. It seemed like it was forever, but within seconds we broke out into clear sky.

I had one of the finest flight instructors. His name was Al, and throughout my training he made sure I experienced every situation that could possibly materialize while in flight. To this day, I attribute our survival of the storm to God, who provided Al to train me in what to do in emergencies. The experience reminds me of Peter walking on the water with Jesus:

> *Now in the fourth watch of the night Jesus went to them, walking on the sea. And when the disciples saw Him walking on the sea, they were troubled, saying, "It is a ghost!" And they cried out for fear. But immediately Jesus spoke to them, saying, "Be of good cheer! It is I; do not be afraid." And Peter answered Him and said, "Lord, if it is You, command me to come to You on the water." So He said, "Come." And when Peter had come down out of the boat, he walked on the water to go to Jesus. But when he saw that the wind was boisterous, he was afraid; and beginning to sink he cried out, saying, "Lord, save me!" And immediately Jesus stretched out His hand and caught him, and said to him, "O you of little faith, why did you doubt?" And when they got into the boat, the wind ceased. (Matthew 14:25-32)*

That summer day at three thousand feet, Jesus made a hole in the clouds and delivered us from harm. Folks need to absorb the precious moments that are filled with precious memories. There is an old gospel song about precious memories and how they linger. If you are in hurry, you will miss them every time. Slowing down will be less stressful and make you happier. And, best of all, you may enjoy the added days to your life.

CHAPTER 2

TROUBLED ABOUT MANY THINGS

I have met people who remind me of a giant red tractor-trailer truck with chrome pipes and a giant sleeper stuck in the mud — the engine turning every rpm the engine can produce, black smoke bellowing out the exhaust stacks like one of the old chimneys down at the Lower Mill in the small town of Pelzer, South Carolina. Mud flying all over the sharp paint job and the shiny chrome wheels. But the sad part is, after expending all that energy, it hasn't moved an inch.

It reminds me of people always in a hurry but never getting anywhere, as illustrated in Luke 10:38-42:

> *Now it happened as they went that He entered a certain village; and a certain woman named Martha welcomed Him into her house. And she had a sister called Mary, who also sat at Jesus' feet and heard His word. But Martha was distracted with much serving, and she approached Him and said, "Lord, do You not care that my sister has left me to serve alone? Therefore tell her to help me." And Jesus answered and said to her, "Martha, Martha, you are worried and troubled about many things. But one thing is needed, and Mary has chosen that good part, which will not be taken away from her."*

Notice what He said in verse 41: "Martha, you are worried and troubled about many things." That is one of our problems today. We suffer from brain overload. You can only manage so many sticks in the fire. You might run around the blazing fire with all the might you possess, but you will never manage them all at the same time. Think about all the things you have to do. Arrange those things in your mind, and you will discover that you can't do everything for everybody at the same time. Slow down, sit down, and relax with a cold glass of iced tea and maybe even a delightful book. Or put on your camouflage and go hunting, or get the boat out and go fishing. You might even want to go to the mall or go out to eat with some friends at a fine restaurant. Get out there and have some fun!

Have you ever heard the story about how to eat an elephant? One bite at the time. That is how you manage life: one day at the time. It is like the gospel song, "One Day at a Time, Sweet Jesus."

Think about it: One day, itself, is enough to negotiate.

CHAPTER 3

SEIZE THE MOMENT

Erma Bombeck said, and I quote: "Remember all those women on the Titanic who waved off the dessert cart."

I have a close friend who frequently uses the words "Life is good." He spends an enormous amount of time traveling with his family, and I assure you he does not let the dessert cart pass by him. He is making every day count. He enjoys every day that God gives him. He said to me once, "Most guys spend their money and time on hobbies and sports; I spend mine on my family." Joe has the recipe for seizing the moment with his family, a trait that is profitable to emulate in our lives as well.

Life is like baseball. Baseball caught my attention in my early years, and I enjoy it to this day. The New York Yankees are my favorite team, and I have always wanted to see Yankee Stadium, located in the Bronx in New York City. A few years ago, my wife and I traveled to New York right before Christmas, and I was blessed to see the stadium. I purchased a real Yankee baseball cap. I am enormously proud of that hat. While visiting there, I could not help but remember the talented players who had played in that great stadium. I could just feel the presence of the men who played there. I could see the Babe pointing to the wall, Mickey Mantle and Roger Maris making the attempt to break the Babe's home run record. I could almost hear Lou Gehrig making his speech at home plate.

I thought about the size of this great edifice and the number of people it would accommodate. Just ordinary folks' young boys glued to the game, watching every move of their favorite player out on the field, along with a few of New York's elite, with giant Cuban cigars clenched between their teeth, enjoying the game. Why, I could even imagine a few nuns down the right field line, screaming with fists clenched as the visiting team's shortstop took a hit away from Bobby Richardson. Yep, those were the golden days.

Baseball reminded me of how many people sit in the stands of life, never getting into the game. In order to play the game, pick up a bat, and pick out one that feels like it is made for your hands. Rub your hand down the bat and feel the smoothness and hardness of the maple wood the bat is made from. Swing it a few times and get used to it. Make it an extension of your body. Next, if you are going to hit the ball and run the bases as the crowd thunders, you have to step up to the plate. When you step up to the plate, throw a little dirt on your hands and rub it in to create a strong grip on the bat.

Now you are ready to play baseball. You take the bat in hand and look into the eyes of the big, strong, talented, athletic pitcher and imagine the pitch coming your way, and then you swing the bat with all the might you can muster. You hear the crack of the bat and watch as the ball climbs higher and higher; you see it disappear over the wall. You begin running the bases because the ball is no longer in the park. The players on the opposing team are standing at their positions with their gloves resting on their hips. The center fielder is standing in front of the "Drink Coca-Cola" sign with a bewildered expression on his face, while the pitcher stands on the red clay mound with his head down. You touch each base with ease and watch as the dust puffs from the bag. Then when you make the turn at third base, and ninety feet away you see home plate. While you are running the last sixty feet, everyone in the crowd is standing on their feet, waving hot dogs and flags and screaming your name. Then you arrive at home plate, where your teammates are waiting to carry you on their shoulders into the dugout. Those last thirty seconds will live on in your mind, and you will share it with your children and grandchildren.

You will never feel the thrill of a great accomplishment sitting in the bleachers.

Get involved! I preach every Sunday about getting involved in the church. There will come a time you will not be able to attend church functions. It may begin by your losing the ability to drive at night, and then your health may fail and you will be confined at home or in some senior home, unable to attend anymore. You have to seize this season in your life before it passes you by.

There is so much you can accomplish in your life through fellowship with fellow Christians. Church is like a filling station, to gas up your life. You leave on a full tank that you can share and with which to make more friends and be a blessing to those around you all week.

Life is worth the living if you seize the moment, regardless of what else is going on. There are so many wonderful and exciting things that God has prepared for each of us here on earth. He created all of it because He intended for us to enjoy it. So get out there and get started. Do something you and your family and friends love to do. Live everyday like it is your last. Don't worry about tomorrow — it has enough problems of its own. Stop worrying, and start enjoying! Jesus said, in Matthew 6:25-32:

> *Therefore I say to you, do not worry about your life, what you will eat or what you will drink; nor about your body, what you will put on. Is not life more than food and the body more than clothing? Look at the birds of the air, for they neither sow nor reap*

nor gather into barns; yet your heavenly Father feeds them. Are you not of more value than they? Which of you by worrying can add one cubit to his stature? So why do you worry about clothing? Consider the lilies of the field, how they grow: they neither toil nor spin; and yet I say to you that even Solomon in all his glory was not arrayed like one of these. Now if God so clothes the grass of the field, which today is, and tomorrow is thrown into the oven, will He not much more clothe you, O you of little faith? Therefore do not worry, saying, "What shall we eat?" or "What shall we drink?" or "What shall we wear?" For after all these things the Gentiles seek. For your heavenly Father knows that you need all these things.

CHAPTER 4

SPEND TIME WITH YOUR CHILDREN

Spend as much time with your children as you can. Life spent with your children is time well spent. Children need guidance; they need structure to teach them how to stand strong in their lives to come.

I have worked in education for many years, and it breaks my heart to see how, generation after generation, the children have less and less support from home. Many take the approach that the school and the church are responsible for raising their children. May I say to you, this approach is not working. Do you want your child to enjoy life and have a good life? Then follow the advice of an old wise king. He said, in Proverbs 22:6, "Train up a child in the way he should go, and when he is old he will not depart from it." He said to train, and that is your obligation as a parent. It is easy for a male and female to have a baby, but it is tough to be the loving and understanding parents the child will need to build a fruitful life.

Parents need to be very vigilant when rearing a child. The first thing to remember is, life and the world are not fair. Our children are going to have to go out into a world that cares not who they are or how they were brought up. There are winners and there are losers, and, believe me, no one wants to be an underdog.

Everyone thinks their child is the greatest child to ever come into the world. Just like everyone else, I think my children are the best. The awkward thing about this: Not all are the best. There are some children who excel more than others. It doesn't make them a better person, and it certainly will not make them more or less successful. This same truth applies to children who do not excel. Some of the greatest minds in history did not always succeed in everything they attempted.

What we fail to tell our children is that, in life, there will be times they will not always enjoy a positive outcome in their endeavors. As parents, we do not want to see our children fail. Most parents will do everything in their power to save them from defeat. However, defeat is as much a part of life as victory. Being defeated is the ultimate teacher. It teaches us that we can be crushed; but it also teaches us to study harder, work harder, pray more, and think more aggressively. God has these words for us in Isaiah 41:10: "Fear not, for I am with you; Be not dismayed, for I am your God. I will strengthen you, Yes, I will help you, I will uphold you with My righteous right hand."

The world is a terrible teacher for children. It is worldly thinking that has brought us to this point in history. Many studies have been done with children from across the globe. The worldly view implies that children who are raised with Christian principles and values are meaner, selfish, and more judgmental. Notice the word judgmental. It is always included in statements when comments are made about Christians. Sound familiar? It should. Our children are being programmed to think like the world. "Put away the truth and make your own" is the way to live. This subject alone could fill and entire library if pursued with rigor.

My advice to parents is to go to church with your children and let your children hear the word of God. Make sure the Bible is available for family readings and discussions. Teach your children to be good morally and to follow the teachings of Christ. Children need proper parental training or they will be like water, just going wherever the current (or crowd) carries them. Once the family is planted on a solid spiritual foundation, the children will be prepared to face and defend themselves from the lies being propagated by those who cherish the world view.

It has progressed to the point of programming our children to believe the untruths, they themselves have come to believe them because of the teaching of others. Programming is a useful tool in the hands of Satan. Unbelievably, it works. Look around you: Nation divided, hate all around us. Jesus said to love your neighbor as yourself. When you learn to listen to the King of kings, you might find out your neighbors are not so bad after all.

A man in the 1930s with a small group of followers led a whole nation astray. Eighty million people listened and did nothing while Adolf Hitler and his Nazi followers took all that Germany was and lost it to the destruction of war. It is amazing how easily he accomplished his sick plan. Like eating an elephant, he started gnawing away at one little piece of freedom at a time. He convinced the youth that his socialist ideas would be a success for both themselves and the country. The Hitler youth were programmed to believe the Nazi philosophy. The entire country was disarmed, books were burned, and church autonomy was no more. Anyone who disagreed with his beliefs was either jailed or faced death at the hands of the Nazi firing squads.

History is one of the most important subjects available for everyone to study. The point of studying history is to help those in the future not make the same mistakes as those before them.

There is one thing about education that I think is worthy information. Many parents today start saving and making plans for the newborn to go to a college or some great university. It is a not a dreadful thing, but some kids are not geared to go to college. Some learn to operate the bulldozer that builds the roads, or become the plumber who fixes pipes, the welder who welds together great buildings. I would wager you didn't know that some of these guys make more than doctors and lawyers. There is no indignity in these professions; these are the people who built America. Without them, I don't know how we would progress or survive.

Have you ever considered the future generations and the skills they will need? My dad taught me how to work on engines and cars and how to farm. My father-in-law taught me plumbing, electrical and HVAC. I built my own house and helped my dad and brother build theirs because an old carpenter taught me how to use a ruler, square, and a level. I am older now and not as able to perform physically as I could when I was younger, but the knowledge has not been lost to time. The things I have learned were not in the halls of some great college. These are skills that young people today cannot perform, and the heartbreaking part is their parents' generations were never exposed to the technical world of hard work.

These skills are important to companies and organizations across this great country we live in. We need to be lifting these skills up to the level of a college degree. Thank God for technical schools and the shop classes in the schools. Remember, one day you are going to need someone to fix your toilet, and if we fail to teach the needed skills you will be on your own.

Proverbs 12:24 says, "The hand of the diligent will rule, but the lazy man will be put to forced labor."

I want you to think about children and technology. There is not a day goes by that I do not see young people walking, driving, or sitting down to eat with a phone or an iPad in hand. Think about when you were young; think about how you know how to do some of the amazing things you do each day. Did you know the greatest inventors in history were dreamers and tinkerers? We want our children to be free thinkers, but we sit idly by while they spend hour after hour glued to their technology. Not only our children, but we, too, need to get out and do some things with our hands. Build something out of nothing. Get your hands dirty. It will wash off with a little soap and water and it will exercise your mind and your body.

So, it is a good thing to save and prepare for your child's future, but let the child have the lead in deciding their professional destiny. If you train them up right and trust God with their lives, there will be no worries about their choice of a vocation. Let them be what they are called to do.

There is another group who thinks their child is going to be a superstar in professional sports. According to the Bureau of Labor Statistics, in 2016 there were 11,800 athletes. Less than five percent of children who play sports will end up on the professional level.

Playing sports is one of the best character builders your child can be involved in. Even though sports are an all-around good activity for children, it will never build the character and moral capacity of Christian teaching. Remember: Your child, just like you, is only passing through this world. Let them know Jesus first, and then sports, and you will have a well-rounded child.

Philippians 4:8 says to us:

Finally, brethren, whatever things are true, whatever things are noble, whatever things are just, whatever things are pure, whatever things are lovely, whatever things are of good report, if there is any virtue and if there is anything praiseworthy — meditate on these things.

The word meditate here gives the impression of an intransitive verb, to think about something carefully, calmly, seriously, and for some time. A person may enjoy the value of this word if it is used to produce sound judgment in practical matters. Down on the farm, we refer to this as good common sense. That, my friend, is a sense you cannot learn on an iPad or a cell phone or in a classroom. It is also a sense that is losing its place to non-sense.

The point here is that young people need to develop their minds and their imaginations by designing their own way of doing things. How many children do you know who have played with a toy they built themselves? How many teenagers do you know who can fix a flat tire on the car their parents have given them to drive? How many young people do you know who can go into the kitchen and prepare a meal without reading a recipe? To some, these are simple things you learned from your parents or some great teacher who took the time to go off the lesson plan and teach some life skills needed to survive.

It would be rewarding for everyone if we stopped spending so much time on technology — precious time that could be used to have a meaningful conversation involving current events, and things we all have the talent to pursue.

Do you ever take the time to look at what your children are doing on their technology? Some, unbelievably, will not look because they feel they are invading the child's privacy. Some folks don't want to know, and then find they are trying to defend their child's action.

There is now the common answer from parents when children get into trouble: "My child wouldn't do that." The truth is we have not a clue what our child might do if we are not around. I have experienced this while working in education. I remember a child who was cursing the bus driver and throwing things at other students on the bus. The child's parents were called to school to view the bus camera video. They sat in their chairs and then replied, "That child in the picture is not mine. He would not do anything like that." I have known parents who threatened their child's teacher because the child's grades were too low for them to enter college. Education is not the big-burger restaurant where you can have it your way. Education has rules, and those rules are there for a purpose. It is our responsibility to govern our children and work with educators for the best outcome for our children.

First Corinthians 13:11 tells us something important about a child: "When I was a child, I spoke as a child, I understood as a child, I thought as a child; but when I became a man, I put away childish things."

Notice the words "understood as a child" and "thought as a child." These are some important words for parents who have a strong belief in child privacy. Listen: Children are just that, children; they think and understand as a child, not as an adult. Parents, whether it is your cup of tea or not, you have to be the parent in the relationship. You must set the tone.

CHAPTER 5

MAKE WORK A JOY

Work should be a fulfilling experience for you. It should be fun and pleasurable; if it is not, you might be in the wrong field. Scripture tells us that if we are to eat, we are to work. First Thessalonians 3:10 says, "For even when we were with you, we commanded you this: If anyone will not work, neither shall he eat." So, if off to work we must go, then let us make it worth the time taken out of our precious lives.

I see so many people who are miserable in their job. The pay is too low, the boss is no good, and "I do all the work because everyone else is on break or gone for the day." They are constantly complaining about their work environment. Listen: If you are suffering under such unbearable surroundings, maybe you should seek other employment. Life is too short, and work too important, to subject ourselves to such unpleasant working conditions.

I have worked in education for well over forty years. It has been a good ride, and I have enjoyed every minute. Sure, there have been some horrible days I would like to put out of mind, but I have wonderful memories that will last me a lifetime.

There was a wonderful man who was the director of operations. He was extremely animated and a fun person to be around. We found there was nothing better than to get something over on him.

The maintenance department was going to lunch at one of the

nearby eating establishments to celebrate an employee's birthday. Someone called Leroy to ask for clearance to go to the luncheon. He said it would be fine as long as "someone" covered the phones. Most folks would never think that answering the phone for an hour could be a challenging task, but the district is the largest in South Carolina, so you can only imagine the number of phone calls placed to the maintenance department on any given day. One of the guys in the office figured that Leroy would be the perfect pick to receive the calls, so he forwarded all the phones to the director's phone.

The luncheon went on without a glitch, but when they returned, the supervisor was summoned to Leroy's office. Both Leroy and his poor secretary were exhausted from the phone duty that had been induced on them. We were all thankful to have a job, but to this day it was worth it.

One day, maintenance received a call concerning a goat some students had tied to the goal post at one of the high schools. I knew Leroy was afraid of farm animals, and since he had called me to take care of the goat situation, I asked the guys to pick up the goat. When they brought the goat back to the shop, on its side was the name of the principal, painted in bright red. I couldn't help myself. When I saw the goat, I told the guys to take it on to Leroy's office, since he was so concerned, and let him see that the goat had been safely removed. They followed my instruction to the letter, and when the goat was led into Leroy's office, he came out of the chair and was standing on the credenza behind his desk, blaring choice words, when I arrived. I never figured out why he was so mad for the rest of the week.

There was a plumber in the department who was bad to overindulge in alcoholic beverages on the weekends. He would come to work on Monday and sleep while the other plumber, his partner, did all the work. One Monday, the other guy, Chuck, had reached the end of the line with his partner's sleeping while he did all the work. While driving back to the shop, our man was still asleep. Chuck saw the train stopped at the grade crossing, waiting to load. Chuck was somewhat of a practical joker, so he fashioned a brilliant idea (and I use the word brilliant lightly). He walked up to the train engineer and asked if he could drive his van up on the track, close to the train engine, and if he would blow the train's big air horns. The engineer agreed to take part in the prank. When the train engineer blew the horn, the sleeping plumber awoke to the sight of giant black-and-white Eastern Seaboard train engine inches from his nose. Until the day he retired, the sleeping plumber never went to sleep on the job again.

During my time with the school district, it was my privilege to work in the energy management department. One of my duties was to survey the schools after hours to assess the number of lights and appliances left on by the staff during the day. It was a lonely job, and sometimes it would be cold out, wandering around schools at night. I decided to take Butch, my boxer, along for the ride and for company. Butch was an exceptionally large dog and somewhat aggressive at times. He picked up on the routine we followed while making the rounds. When I would open a door, he would dart into the darkness beyond the door and then come back and let me know everything was clear.

One night we were checking a small Florida-style elementary school, where all the doors opened to the outside. I opened the first door, and Butch, as usual, went into the room first; except this time there was a loud and dreadful noise. You could hear the chairs being shoved while the dog was making the most ferocious growling sound. I thought he was in attack mode. Reaching into the room to turn the light, I could see his victim. The teacher had been teaching biology, and hanging from the ceiling was a full-size human skeleton. Butch had torn the unfortunate thing apart and scattered it all over the classroom. We spent the rest of the night putting that skeleton back together. I could have choked Butch. He just sat there watching me as I tried to figure which bone fit the other. (I think somebody wrote a song about which bone was attached to the other.) It was another memory posted to the files of my mind. Every time I see a boxer, I think about Butch; he was a great dog and companion.

I was playing in a golf tournament with a few men from work. One of them was a great person; you could always count on him when the chips were down. But his golfing abilities were somewhat questionable. I noticed, as we played along, he kept slicing the ball into the trees. I said to him, "Ross, you need a different driver. The one you have is no good." He looked at me as if I had insulted his beloved driver, which he had purchased for five dollars out of some barrel at the Salvation Army. On the next hole, he sliced his ball right into the lake. My playing partner and I drove our cart over beside Ross as he gazed into the deep murky pond where his ball had come to rest. I reached into my bag and took a driver that had changed my game. I propped it on my cart and walked over and took Ross's out of his bag and threw it in the pond. The look on his face was worth a million dollars. He said, "Boss, that is the only driver I have, and we still have the back nine to play." He never got mad or upset. His attitude never changed. I reached behind me, took the driver, and gave it to him. He didn't slice another ball.

I finished my service at the district with one of the best secretaries anyone could have. She was a godsend in my life. It was her passion to argue with me. I will miss those times with her. She was, however, prone to be in the wrong place at the wrong time. We had a genuine problem in the security dispatch area. A panic button had been pressed for test at the district office. The alarm was not responded to, which, to say the least, raised the blood pressure of those performing the test. Cindy had wandered into the area on one of her social visits when the test signal sounded in the security area. Of course, the failure to respond was immediately brought to everyone's attention. It was an important event. It was about the safety of employees at the location. It could have been real, and people could have been in great danger.

I asked the supervisor to check the cameras in the area to see what could have led to the alarm being ignored. A few hours later, the supervisor called me and said, "I am not sure exactly what happened, but I don't think you are going to be pleased with what the camera has revealed." So, of course, I asked him to proceed. He said, "Just let me send you the footage and you can see for yourself."

As I watched the footage, lo and behold, there was Cindy, standing in the middle of the floor, having the time of her life — socializing, laughing, and swinging her arms around — entertaining the folks who were supposed to be answering the alarm. You would have thought she was in a vaudeville show. Have you ever had one of those days when you wished you had stayed in bed?

There are fun things at work, but there are blessings too. There were days I visited the schools to talk with principals and custodians about needs they might have. Each time, I was blessed to see students of all ages engaged in the learning process. It was pleasant to hear about teachers, principals, custodians, food service folks, and bus drivers who went the extra mile in caring for the needs of some student and, in more than one instance, multiple students. These occurrences reminded me of how Jesus cared for the people around Him while He walked this earth.

I was extremely proud of one of our district directors because of a story he shared with the executive team. It happened at the Friday night football game. A player was injured, and the ambulance was called to attend to the player. While waiting for the paramedics to check the young man's condition before placing him in the ambulance to transport him to the hospital, one of the referees asked the young man's parents if he could pray with their son. The parents agreed, and the referee and the other referees calling the game surrounded the boy as he lay on green grass and began to pray. When they were finished, the EMTs began loading the player into the ambulance. His body had been numbed by the injury, and his coordination was compromised. He could not get up, nor could he walk. Before the ambulance left the stadium, it stopped, and the young player came out of the vehicle and walked back to the home side of the field. God answers prayers — sometimes quickly, and other times over time. He is faithful and can be trusted with any problem we may have. Jesus said, in Matthew 18:19-21: "Again I say to you that if two of you agree on earth concerning anything that they ask, it will be done for them by My Father in heaven. For where two or three are gathered together in My name, I am there in the midst of them."

I shall never forget a young man I hired through a special program one summer when he was fourteen years of age. He was a skinny little guy with a deep voice. He wore these large black-rim glasses. He had very fair skin and unmanageable red hair with noticeable cow licks around the crown of his head. His clothes were not the best, but he had a proud look on his face and a good attitude. He was an industrious worker but needed to be shown what to do because this was his first job and he had little experience. Everyone liked Randy, and he merged right in with the full-time crew. Before long, he received the nickname Frog, because of his deep voice and small frame.

He did tend to get into mischief on occasion. One of the regular custodians rode a little scooter to work. He was so proud of that little red scooter, and he took such loving care of it. As I arrived at school one morning, I noticed something odd hanging on the flagpole in front of the school. As I walked to the office, I could not believe my eyes. There was Lee's scooter hanging at the top of the flagpole. I called the entire team to the front of the school, and I watched the expression on the faces of each one as they looked up and saw the bike dangling. Only one of them didn't look up. Randy tried to act as though he didn't know the thing was up there. I was furious, because that was the only thing Lee had for transportation, and there it was swinging in the wind. I was thankful it wasn't harmed, but Randy incurred my wrath for the rest of the day.

He would work, and work hard; he just didn't want to go home after work. A brief time later, I learned he had been thrown out of the house by his father, who was abusive. He had ended up with a neighbor who took him in. The conditions were not good, but it gave him a roof over his head and food to eat. They would bring him to school and pick him up after work in a huge, bright green Cadillac with whip antennas mounted on the bumper. It would embarrass Randy so much when other students saw him getting in the vehicle.

I recommended him later for a full-time job. He excelled as a custodian. Randy knew what clean was, and he made sure his area and the areas of his co-workers were clean. He worked hard and gained more confidence, excelling to the point that he was promoted to a supervisory position. Today he supervises twenty-five schools. He has a college degree and is happily married. He is a devoted Christian and a man of integrity.

It is because of Randy's accomplishments that I have little patience for folks who want to blame their parents and their past for the problems they have in life. He is an example of a proven overcomer. First John 5:5 explains this well: "Who is he who overcomes the world, but he who believes that Jesus is the Son of God?" And 1 John 4:4 says, "You are of God, little children, and have overcome them, because He who is in you is greater than he who is in the world."

There was a dark time in my career with the district when someone started a horrible rumor that I was abusing my position. The story was that I was using district personnel to work on my private land on district time. The rumor mill grew at an enormous pace, until one day the superintendent intervened. He appointed an investigator to find the truth. I never knew at the time that the investigation was in progress. When it was all said and done, I was cleared of any wrongdoing. I cannot count the times I have thanked "The Boss" for taking this action. That was the last time I ever heard anyone mention anything about the rumor. I think God was in charge, and it was overseen professionally and to the point. It wasn't a good memory, but it is an experience I shall never forget.

The superintendent and his wife, Tina, are two of the greatest people you would ever want to meet. He is a very gifted individual. There are few individuals who are highly educated and have good common sense, as he does. I have learned many of life's lessons from this man and will cherish the memory.

Now, he, too, has his moments. One cold and freezing morning, we were riding to check the roads. We did this every time there was severe weather predicted for the Greenville area. He and I had met at the central office, when he said, "Ride with me, we need to check some more streets." Now, I really had no intention of going anywhere but home, because conditions were worsening quickly. I sat down in his vehicle, closed the door, and he started down every street he could find. Later we would learn this was one of the worse ice storms in a long time in the Upstate of South Carolina, and there we were right in the middle of it. Giant limbs from the old oak trees were breaking from the weight of the ice right in front of the vehicle as he showed off his cat-like reflexes. Transformers on the power lines were exploding and power lines were striking the road, sending off sparks like the Fourth of July, and I am thinking, "Why in the world did I get into this car?"

When it comes to weather, The Boss gets excited like a kid in a candy store. He is an active, personal-participation kind of person. We never had a superintendent who would get out in the trenches with us.

He loves to check behind you. He always told me, "Trust but verify," and, my goodness, would he verify.

On one of the snowy days, part of the team headed by the same guy who transferred all the phones to the director's office had his team off the side of one of the roads near the mountains in the northern section of the county. They were all reporting from the same spot. These ole boys were spinning yarns and having an enjoyable time while the downpour of snow was covering the roads quickly. They had no idea the superintendent was creeping up slowly but deliberately on their little party. I don't believe in all the years that Monty and I worked together that he had contrived a taller tale than he did for the superintendent on that cold frosty morning on the side of the highway in the foothills of the Blue Ridge Mountains.

CHAPTER 6

THE PLAGUE

W hile I was writing this book, a major catastrophe struck America and the world. The coronavirus (Covid 19) originated in China and quickly spread to the rest of the world. Quarantines, travel restrictions, social distancing, and masks became the norm for protection against this terrible virus. Many have died, and many more, I am afraid, will meet the same destiny. If faith in God and prayer are important at any time, now is the time.

People are in a constant state of panic because one of our greatest and trusted resources, the news media, have propagated fear across the globe. The agencies we once trusted to give unbiased reporting of events are now using opinionated reporting and are hiding truth, producing division and panic in our great nation. The Bible says this in Proverbs 14:5: "An honest witness does not deceive, but a false witness pours out lies" (NIV). News reporters should be forthright in presenting their stories to the public.

It is my opinion that if you are going to release something to the public, make it the undeniable truth. My dad used to say the truth can stand on its own foundation while a lie will need further lying to keep it afloat. His statement was correct when he said it, and it is still true today.

I have been amazed at the outpouring of misinformation during the coronavirus crisis. Wrong information has led to conspiracy theories and even demonstrations in the streets. I am not downplaying the effects of the virus, because so many are dying every day. The economy has crashed, and many have no jobs. Many have no food to eat and are depending on churches and other groups to feed them each day.

I have thought about the hand of God's imminent judgment during this exceedingly difficult time. The Scriptures are quite unambiguous concerning God's judgment of sin. I have considered the state of the human race and our existing mindsets. In America we have killed millions of babies by abortion, with no remorse. According to Fox News, New York and Virginia legislatures passed late-term abortion measures that are seen by many, even on the pro-choice side, to be too extreme. Parents are killing and abusing their own children.

Sins that have been clearly stated in both the Old and New Testament have been renamed "alternative lifestyles." If you think it's okay, and the world thinks it is okay, do it. As a pastor, it breaks my heart that so many are being deceived by Satan, the great deceiver and the father of all lies. Jesus said to the Pharisees in John 8:44, "You are of your father the devil, and the desires of your father you want to do. He was a murderer from the beginning, and does not stand in the truth, because there is no truth in him. When he speaks a lie, he speaks from his own resources, for he is a liar and the father of it."

There are many ways to God. Why is Christianity the only way? In John 14:6-7, Jesus said, "I am the Road, also the Truth, also the Life. No one gets to the Father apart from me. If you really knew me, you would know my Father as well. From now on, you do know him. You've even seen him!" (MSG). Jesus is the only way; there is no other way to God.

Drugs and child-trafficking are out of hand, with thousands of young people missing or dying from overdoses because of the trafficking issue.

Our representatives in Washington are more concerned with their greed for money and power than for the people they serve. Greed, of course, leads to additional sin, in our quest to satisfy our flesh. First John 2:16 says, "For everything in the world — the lust of the flesh, the lust of the eyes, and the pride of life — comes not from the Father but from the world."

God hates sin, but there is no doubt He loves every one of us, demonstrating it when He gave His only son as a sacrifice for the sins of man. What breaks my heart is that time is going to run out for many, and it will be too late.

I am afraid, as Christians, we have become too much like the world, so much so you cannot tell the Christians from the rest. Churches have lost their direction and have become little more than country clubs. Pastors in the pulpits across the globe are preaching soothing messages to soothe the hearts of the people under the hearing of their words. Pastors have cowered in the face of public pressure and failed to preach the Bible in its fullness. Many pastors are no longer Spirit-led, but are controlled by popularity and riches. They are afraid to preach that abortion is murder and that homosexuality is an abomination. They are afraid to preach that God created a male and a female, and what the Scripture says does not declare approval to change the sex a person is born with.

People have listened to the deceptive lies of their father, Satan. They want to be the god of their lives; they want to make their own choices about what is right and what is wrong. I know that people reading this chapter may think my thoughts are offensive. So be it; I had rather you be offended than to die and go to a real place called hell.

Our representatives and leaders have been deceived by these same lies. They, with the assistance of our news agencies, have propagated the lies to the point the country is divided into two categories: the left and the right. Partisanship is no longer practiced. Both sides refuse to meet in the middle on anything. Mark 3:25 says, "If a house is divided against itself, that house cannot stand" (NIV). You will remember that Abraham Lincoln used this portion of Scripture in a speech on June 16, 1858, at a Republican convention.

Christians have been placed on the far right because of our conservative beliefs — beliefs, may I say, that this great country was founded on. Some say, not so; these are the people who are trying to rewrite the history books and abolish the Constitution.

If you should take the time to do some serious research on American history, you would find that, in fact, this country was founded on Christian principles and that a majority of our forefathers were great men of God who believed the Bible and believed that prayer was a necessary part of their lives. There is an astounding difference between the authentic history of these great statesmen and what some write about them today. No, they were not perfect; they made mistakes, some serious mistakes, because, like you and I, they were humans. They were sinners who accepted Jesus Christ as Lord of their lives. Any statements concerning the lives of these great men can only rest on historical facts, which does not allow us to be appointed judges of their character or their religious beliefs.

I am extremely proud of our church. Folks have stepped up freely and given of their time to prepare meals and pass them out to the hungry. The school district has fed thousands of meals to children.

At the beginning of the pandemic, everything was closed, including churches, across the land. Services were streamed via Internet. I noticed people reaching out to God during those uncertain times. This is a normal and a universal reaction when danger and fear are present. In the book of Judges in the Old Testament, you can see, as the cloud of hopelessness lingered over the heads of the people of Israel, they would immediately seek the God of Israel to come to their aid. They were people just like us. They feared for their lives. They never figured out, as we have not today, that we need to have a daily walk with God and not just try to find Him when the dark clouds of tribulations have amassed over our lives.

I observed the viewer count on our church's online services. At the beginning of the pandemic, it was in the thousands of viewers, but as the government began relaxing the restrictions in order to reopen the economy, the viewership began to decline. Just like the people of Israel, as things get better, the need for God becomes less important. When will mankind realize a daily relationship with Jesus Christ is our only hope?

CHAPTER 7

A GOOD ATTITUDE IS ONE
OF LIFE'S BLESSINGS

A caring attitude is a necessity in the Christian walk. We read in Matthew 9:36, "But when He saw the multitudes, He was moved with compassion for them, because they were weary and scattered, like sheep having no shepherd."

Most of the successful men and women I have met over the years have a servant attitude. There was a deputy superintendent who was with the school district for a few years. Mason was a great Christian man; he had a love for God that all Christians should imitate. He was as big as a mountain and strong as an ox, but his attitude was one of servitude.

He has a beautiful family, and they live on a small Ponderosa-like ranch in a neighboring county (you know — one of those spreads with a registered herd of cattle grazing in large lustrous pastures with fancy white fencing). His house is large and beautiful. It sets off the landscape of the farm, which is divided by a highway that bears his family name.

He does have a beautiful family — a beautiful wife, a handsome son and two beautiful daughters (one of whom has suffered with some bone problems, but she has shown her faith in the Lord through all the pain she endured).

He loves the Lord, and you can see it in his actions. He has never met a stranger and never had a harsh word. He is one of those people who would set you straight, and you would not know he did until you got in the car to return to the office. I was in his office one day talking about a problem. At the end of the conversation, he stood up and said, "Do I have to come over there and fix it myself?" He was kidding, but the moment has been embedded in my mind since then.

Now, this guy can eat, and he loved to go to a restaurant that specialized in the best hot dogs you have ever tasted. I would bring one of my guys and pick him up, and away we would go down to "Skins." Mason would go in and immediately begin poor-mouthing and asking for discounts, to which the ladies would smile and tell him to sit down. He and B.T. would start the meal with five dogs and order follow-ups. I do not believe I have ever seen anyone who could equal the appetite of those two.

Right after his retirement, he received some news that would have been devastating to most people. The doctor told him he had found some problems with his colon that had the appearance of cancer. Mason stood before the news just as David stood before Goliath. His faith never foundered, and when the surgery was complete there was no sign of disease. His Christlike attitude gave him victory.

Life is about attitude, which can be illustrated by this story, which can be found at ministry127.com:

The noted English architect Sir Christopher Wren was supervising the construction of a magnificent cathedral in London. A journalist thought it would be interesting to interview some of the workers, so he chose three and asked them this question: "What are you doing?" The first replied, "I'm cutting stone for ten shillings a day." The next answered, "I'm putting in ten hours a day on this job." But the third said, "I'm helping Sir Christopher Wren construct one of London's greatest cathedrals."

There is a man who attends my church. He is a deacon and Sunday school teacher. He is married to a young lady I have known for decades. I must tell you about this couple because they are so inspiring.

Curt was a great electrician and worked hard. One night, coming home from a race in Charlotte, North Carolina, he was involved in a serious automobile accident. The car flipped, throwing him out of the car. The car landed on him and paralyzed him from the chest down. Bound to a wheelchair, he maintained an attitude of hope. Most people would have let their attitude fall to the bottom of the barrel and turn into an invalid, but not Curt; no sir, he knew his condition was traumatic, but he was bullishly determined.

He and his wife asked Jesus into their lives later and become members of our fellowship. When he came out of the baptismal pool, he was a determined man. He began to study God's word every day, and it wasn't long until he began to put the chapters and verses to memory. Even to this day, it is incredible how he can recite to you the chapter and verse and, most times, what it says. He is my best friend, with whom I spend hours talking and sometimes arguing about Scripture and current events. He is very argumentative at times, so much so that I call him a cantankerous old goat.

He and his wife were young when the accident took place. Curt hadn't been the best of husbands and had given Sonja a challenging time before the accident. I have told Curt on several occasions that God gave him an angel to be his wife, and he agrees. She has stood by his side and cared for his needs all these years, and his needs are many and require a lot of time and a lot of strength. When the pastor said, "In sickness and health," she meant it when she said, "I will." She, too, is involved in our church, and she is a wonderful decorator and cook. They have adopted a beautiful child and they continue choosing a good attitude over a bad one.

The attitude decision is yours when you rise from your bed each morning. You can see the beautiful day that God has given you, and you can decide without delay that life is going to be good at work, at school, or at home. Or you can choose to make yourself miserable, and everyone around you too.

There was a cranky grandpa who stretched out on the couch one afternoon for his nap. While he slept, his grandson carefully applied some Limburger cheese to his mustache. Grandpa awoke with a snort and grumbled, "This room stinks." He walked from room to room and finally said, "This whole house stinks." He went outside and cried, "The entire world stinks!"

Many are like Grandpa; they think everything, and everybody, stinks. The reality is, carrying a bad attitude makes you stink, and everyone around you knows it.

Your attitude can make or break you; nothing is more important than having a good, positive attitude. Your attitude can make your marriage miserable, or it can produce a happy and exciting union for a man and a woman. Your attitude can give you peace at work or ruin you as an employee. It can be the difference between failure and success. It can be a boost to your Christian walk, or it can destroy it. Your attitude between you and God can send you to heaven or it can send you to hell. How about your attitude? What is your attitude with God?

According to medical doctors, there is a substantial number of cancer patients who have beaten the terrible disease because of their faith and attitude. There is not anything in the world more pleasurable than hanging out with a person with a good attitude. You seem to never forget them.

When I was growing up, my best friend was an example of a good attitude. He was born with congenital talipes equinovarus (clubfoot). Keith went through numerous surgeries at the Shriners Hospital, and not once did you ever hear him complain. We played baseball together, and he was a baseball dictionary. He could name every player on most of the Major League teams.

During this time, I had a kidney disorder as a result of red measles, which confined me to bed rest for many months. I could see Keith out my bedroom window, coming around the curve on our road with a big smile on his face and his eyes sparkling. You could see the love of life just bursting out of him like my grandmother's spring flowers popping out of the ground. He would come into my room and trade baseball cards and talk about the game we were watching on the little black-and-white television my brother and I shared.

He introduced me to Clemson football. We would listen to the games on the radio and watch them on the television when the game had coverage. Keith loved to read the team's statistics every Sunday while I read the funny paper. He loved him some Tigers, and because of him they have remained my favorite team until this day.

I think a lot about Keith. He died unexpectedly several years ago, but the memories we made together have persevered in my thoughts. When he passed, the memories bubbled in my mind like the fizz in a soda. The thought came to my mind of how he could have been out with other kids, playing ball and having the time of his life. But he chose to hang out with me. I loved him like a brother, and I will never forget him. He was the epitome of a true friend.

CHAPTER 8

GOOD MEMORIES ARE IMPORTANT

A part of life is making memories! Memories are important; they recall the good things, and sometimes the terrible things, we have experienced along the way.

I remember my wife, Rhonda, putting together a family vacation to the Bahamas. She worked tirelessly for weeks to make sure everything would be perfect for everyone. The day arrived for us to leave for Florida, where we would be staying in this wonderful hotel with a pool and palm trees all around.

The arrival at the inn was a day that will live in infamy for the entire family. It was the worst place you could imagine to be a patron. It was nothing like the pictures, and there must have been only one cleaning person. We looked at each other in the car, and you could see the beaming, happy, and excited faces begin to melt into the moment of total letdown. We, of course, found a more suitable place with clean beds and running water.

The next morning, we were to board the ship for the cruise to the Bahamas. It was then we found we had to listen to a boring two-hour spiel about timeshares. I believe it was the longest and most horrible two hours before we were awarded our free tickets (I use the word "free" lightly). After this grueling day, we felt things would move to the positive side of life. However, the timeshare presentation was only the preamble for the rest of the trip.

We sailed the next morning, and it was beautiful. The Atlantic Ocean was lovely. The water was so blue, and the dolphins were entertaining the group as we made our way to our destination. I could only think of how God had prepared this incredible scene for us thousands of years ago, and we were viewing it as a family, including my four-year-old grandson Ellison (a.k.a. "The Dickster"). He was captivated by the size of the ship and the fun things he was privileged to do. There is not anything better than to watch a four-year-old on his first cruise. He was so inquisitive. He had more questions than Carter made liver pills. He was just a wild child having the time of his life as we sailed to our destination.

We arrived at port early the next morning. We had been on other cruises, but my eyes had never seen the sight that was before them that morning. The place looked abandoned! We all turned and looked at Rhonda with the same gaze we mustered up at the hotel. The crew shuffled us off the ship and through customs and into a cab that looked as if it had been driven to the island from New York through the ocean.

Arrival at the resort only brought more. Rooms were not ready until 9:00 p.m. I began to wonder what in the world I was doing there. We were in the lobby, trying to get keys to our condominium. People were losing their temper, shouting at the top of their lungs. I felt so sorry for the folks at the desk who had to listen to this obnoxious group of people. Somebody had it coming, but not these folks.

We had a beautiful day on the beach, living out of our suit cases. The beach and the water were beautiful. The water was calm as a farm pond, and the color was as blue as the sky. You could feel the warm, gentle wind as it caressed your body, scorching in the midday sun. Even though we couldn't get to our rooms, the day was beautiful and the experience refreshing.

We went to wander through the shops and grab some supper. I went into a little gift shop. The clerk came up to me, and we began a lengthy conversation. She was proud to tell me she had visited our great country and how well she was treated during her vacation. I could not resist asking about her relationship with Jesus Christ. She was not shy and immediately told me she attended church with her mother on occasion but never really received anything while there. She went on to say she was looking for something real in her life, something she could wrap her arms around. "Jesus," I said, "is what you are trying to find." She asked, "If this is so, how do I discover His whereabouts?"

It was at that moment I realized why I was in the Bahamas. I explained the salvation that our Lord had suffered and paid for. She prayed and asked Jesus into her life that night. Through a veil of tears, she thanked me for bringing Him with me. I forgot the roller coaster ride we had experienced while coming to the island and was humbled that God had used me to bring this wonderful human being into the family of God. (Later, one night while watching the news, I learned that Hurricane Dorian had destroyed the island. I was concerned and wondered if she had survived the terrible hurricane. It was comforting to know she had found Jesus.)

We left a few days later and began our trip back to beautiful, sunny South Carolina. I know this seems to be a long story, but we have shared so many laughs and praises about this vacation. Even the impoverished things in life can be a wonderful memory to cherish.

CHAPTER 9

PUT THE PAST IN THE PAST

Your past can be a demon that constantly tries to ruin your life. It is Satan's greatest tool to continually discredit your life. There is nothing he loves better than to deceive you into thinking that, because of your past, you are tarnished and unreliable. You think if people only knew, they would never look at you the same again.

I am the pastor of a wonderful church. It is the church I grew up in. I have loved this church, and the people have loved me, all my life. But I failed God, my family, my children, my wife, and my church. I pondered writing this chapter and exposing the bad choices that I made and the results of those choices. I hope my experience will, in some way, help someone else who may invite the thought of traveling the road to destruction I traveled.

I married my high school sweetheart when I was eighteen years of age. We did not have anything. We lived in a mobile home on a busy highway that her dad financed for us. We were so young, and so petted, by our parents. We were very childish and immature.

I went to basic training in 1969, only a year after we were married. During that time, I began to wander into places I should never have been. I will never forget Fort Bragg, North Carolina, and the city right outside the gates of the fort, Fayetteville. It was a place of intrigue for a young country boy who had lived on a farm with strict parents and grandparents. My new Army buddies and I frequented most all the topless bars along the strip, drinking our fill of beer and liquor. We would be drunk out of our minds when the taxi dropped us off back at the barracks.

I remember sitting on the steps with one of my fellow recruits, trying to lead him to the Lord. He was listening. He was taking in every word. He said, "I want to talk about that some more tomorrow." That was on a Saturday. That night we went over to the 82nd Airborne club, where I got so drunk I didn't wake up until Sunday afternoon. The guy never mentioned our conversation again.

After I came home from active duty, my wife and I moved to the city (or may I say town, because it was so small). Williamston was a beautiful place to call home. It has a park with a natural spring. The water flowing from this beautiful little spring is said to have healing powers because of the minerals contained in the water. Folks would come from everywhere just to drink the water produced by the little spring.

The park that surrounds the spring is filled with great southern oaks and pines. Families would come in the spring and fall to celebrate their family reunions. Folks would gather under the trees and spread the tables with country cooking that would melt in your mouth. There would be fried chicken and mashed potatoes, and it didn't arrive in a box. The Pepsi and Coke in glass bottles — and, yes, the sweet tea and lemonade — would be flowing while the musically talented members of the family would play gospel and country music while the family sang along.

I took a job with the local furniture store and attended National Guard drills each month. We lived in a mobile home located on Dove Street. I was working on appliances and installing air-conditioning. We were young and had no idea what we were doing. I am thankful we had no children during that period.

It wasn't long until our first child was born; we named him Johnathan and called him Jay. Nicknames are a family thing; everyone has one. He was a beautiful child. We were living with my parents and were financially in good shape. My wife had taken a great job with the state, and I was working for the school district and serving with the National Guard and moonlighting on appliances and HVAC. We seemed to be on our way.

We decided to build our own home. We started it in 1974 and finished it on Christmas Eve, 1977, and moved in. It took me and an old carpenter three years to build our dream home. It was so nice. It was a joy to be on our own. Life was simply perfect for nine years.

We were attending church. She and I both were teaching Sunday school, and I was serving on the deacon board. Jay had accumulated several perfect attendance pins for Sunday school. We were living the dream, and life was good. In 1984 our beautiful daughter was born, and we named her Caroline. ("Business" is her nickname, because she is always tending to someone's activities.) We had a wonderful home and a wonderful relationship.

It was during this time that I made some horrible personal choices that destroyed our marriage. I had wondered often how David, a man after God's own heart, could possibly have allowed himself to become attracted to a woman outside of his marriage. I had read that story many times and thought it could never happen to me. But it did. I ruined my relationship with my wife and children and lost all respect people might have had for me. I hurt my children and my parents. My children suffered the most, and only in the last few years has God restored our relationships.

I have learned through this experience why God hates divorce. Malachi spoke these words in chapter 2, verse 16: "For the Lord God of Israel says that He hates divorce, for it covers one's garment with violence."

Divorce creates problems that wound the heart — all the way to the soul. My experience reminds me of the prodigal son, who wandered away but one day came to himself. When I came to myself, it was too late to fix the mess I had made.

God hates divorce, but He loves you and me. Like David, we, too, can be forgiven for this mistake, as well as any and all sins we have committed, if we seek His forgiveness and repent of our sins.

First John 1:9 says, "If we confess our sins, He is faithful and just to forgive us our sins and to cleanse us from all unrighteousness." That is a promise!

Once you feel God's hand of forgiveness on you, it is time to put away the old and look forward to the new. Paul said in Philippians 3:13-14, "Brethren, I do not count myself to have apprehended; but one thing I do, forgetting those things which are behind and reaching forward to those things which are ahead, I press toward the goal for the prize of the upward call of God in Christ Jesus."

Many have experienced the same thing in their lives and are constantly tormented by the decision. The path you tread after divorce is not a pleasant journey. That is the reason when I counsel so many married couples on the verge of divorce, I tell them what lies ahead if they take this step. God knew the pain and suffering his children would go through when He gave these words to Malachi to pass along to us. Jesus would later reinforce these words to the Jews. Over the years, I have experienced and seen the disasters that have injured families because of divorce. It not only affects non-believers, but Christians, as well.

There is one way, and only one way, to avoid a broken home, and that is to put Jesus in the center of the home. I know you have heard the quote "A family that prays together stays together." There is a lot of truth in that quote. Keep God in the marriage, and when things get tough or out of hand, look to Him for reconciliation. I will assure you: He knows better than anyone how to keep the knot tied and the family together.

CHAPTER 10

TRIALS AND TRIBULATIONS OF LIFE

Sickness came into our home in 2004. Rhonda was diagnosed with breast cancer. My wandering eyes and thoughts stopped, but my drinking didn't; I thought I could not make it through all of this without it. She suffered for two years with treatments and side effects. It destroyed me every day. Finally, she was pronounced cancer-free.

You never know how much you love someone until the moment comes when you think you are going to lose them. I have preached funerals and watched adult children who were so busy that they had no time for Mother and Daddy come to the point where they crave another day, another hour, or even a few minutes just to tell them how much they really loved them. It is the saddest time a person can experience. Many will spend years trying to get through the grieving process. That is the reason you need to spend time with the people you love. Give them a big hug and tell how much you love them.

My life was only partially changed through Rhonda's cancer. God had more work to do. In April 2008 I was diagnosed with colorectal cancer. It had progressed to stage three. The gastroenterologist who did the colonoscopy came to my bedside and said, "You have a large tumor in your rectum, and because of its size it has been present for quite some time."

When Rhonda and I arrived home, I announced to my family the test results. Tears were shed. My brother Cooter was broken. That was on a Friday, and the next day Cooter came to me and said, "Let's go up to the church and get down on the altar, because you are going to have to talk to God and listen to what He tells you to do."

When we arrived at the church, my brother began to pray. His prayer was so powerful, I felt lightning might strike us dead at any moment. I knelt on that altar and I confessed every miserable and disgusting sin I had ever committed, and I begged — I mean begged — God for forgiveness. And then … I felt His forgiveness immediately. God did it right there on the spot. I could feel His hand, I could feel the touch. He had restored my soul. From that moment, I never again entertained the notion that I was going to die from my cancer.

When I met with the surgeon a week later, he told me he had reviewed the pictures of the tumor and did not believe it was as large as the other doctor thought. The tumor was smaller than first diagnosed. He was incredibly positive and told me he had a plan to stop the disease.

I went through thirty-seven chemo and radiation treatments before having three surgeries. On a followup visit to Dr. Rex's office, he took out a calendar from the top his mahogany desk. The calendar had pictures of twelve people, one for each month of the year. They looked so healthy, and most had been doing some serious bodybuilding. All of them had been diagnosed with the same cancer I had. He said to me, "Dicky, this calendar was last year's. All these people who look so healthy are dead." I was speechless. I could not open my mouth.

On the way home, I thought my past had finally caught up to me. I figured I probably had only a year, at the most, to live. I didn't tell anyone what he told me. I just held it in, waiting for that dreaded day when the cancer would return, just as it had with those twelve people on the pages of that calendar. I was broken! But as I continued to drive, I turned on the radio. A pastor was preaching from Acts 3:6: "Then Peter said, 'Silver and gold I do not have, but what I do have I give you: In the name of Jesus Christ of Nazareth, rise up and walk.'" Immediately these words came to me: "With men it is impossible, but not with God; for with God all things are possible."

The surgeries were successful, and the cancer was removed from my body. I was cancer-free, but so were the people on that calendar. My oncologist wanted to give me a regimen of chemotherapy to kill any cancer cells that might still be lingering in by body.

In July of 2009, the chemotherapy treatment meant to poison the lingering cancer cells, poisoned me. I was placed in ICU at the hospital, my body functions shutting down. My family was called in. My coworkers came to say their farewells. The nurses were asking Rhonda and my two children if they wanted life support or not. For three weeks, I lay in a comatose condition, until one morning I awoke in a room with the sun shining so bright.

My view was so clear, and I felt no pain. Rhonda had gone home to get a shower and asked Sonja to stay with me until she returned. (Sonja is the wife of Curt, and they both are two of the greatest friends a family could have.) She took me out into the wellness court. It was wonderful to smell the flowers and plants and to breathe again the clean air God provides. It was a wonderful feeling to know that God had spared my life.

A few weeks later I was declared cancer-free by Dr. Gococo. He is one of the best oncologists in the world. Over the years, we saw him so much that Rhonda and I treated him as our family doctor. He has the most interesting personality and loves to use illustrations to explain the treatment plans he has for you.

There was a dear lady in our congregation who retired on a Tuesday and was diagnosed with cancer on Wednesday. (Kind of makes you think twice about retirement, does it not?) She went through a terrible ordeal. Her husband called me one day and said Peggy is giving up and wants to die. On the way to hospital I prayed for the right words to say to her.

At the hospital, she was lying in the bed with her family surrounding her. She told me, "I want Jesus to come and get me, because I just can't take this anymore." I told her, "We can't make that decision. It belongs to God, and if you are still here, he has more for you to do in this life. No one is dying today. I want you to take Jesus by the hand and start fighting this disease right now."

She looked at me with eyes that were weak with suffering from the traumatic surgery she had undergone. "I am going to fight," she said. And fight, she did. She is alive as I write these words and has become a real trouper for the Lord. She still has problems from the surgery, but she just keeps on keeping on.

You would think that what Peggy had been through would have been enough for one family to manage. But while she was hospitalized, her husband was admitted to the hospital with a heart problem. I visited Kent at the hospital. The doctors found that his heart was out of rhythm. He stayed a week until they figured out a solution to set his rhythm back to normal. Thanks be to God for his wonderful grace! Both Peggy and Kent returned to normal lives.

We can't step out of life like we would step off an airplane. Life goes on until God says it is over. During times of trouble, we should trust God with the outcome. Hebrews 13:5 tells us, "Let your conduct be without covetousness; be content with such things as you have. For He Himself has said, 'I will never leave you nor forsake you.'"

I was at the hospital with another dear lady when the doctor came out after surgery and said that she had cancer but there was nothing he could do surgically to extract the cancer. Her husband and I looked at each other in dismay. She never missed a beat. She said, "There will be a way." She made an appointment with an oncologist, who recommended treatments. The church prayed for her, and the treatments were successful. She had a few bouts with the cancer returning in various places, but she continued with a good attitude. She rarely missed church, and she loved going to the beach.

It wasn't long after her diagnosis that she and her husband received a phone call informing them their youngest daughter had overdosed and died. The family was shocked, as was the church family. I was so upset that drugs had taken the life of such a beautiful child. I observed this family as they weathered this storm in their life. They had already lost their youngest son in an accidental shooting. I began to wonder just how much one family could endure.

As time passed, both Karen and Jim held tight to their faith. Not once did they blame God for the storms in their life. They stood together in the torrent and the frigid wind, following Jesus out of the storm. The experience made them both stronger in their faith.

It was not long until Karen's cancer returned, and she, too, passed away. Jim now spends an enormous amount of his time working in the church and helping people in need.

God uses these trials in our lives to make us stronger and more faithful Christians. Trials noticeably change the lives of those who pass through them. Romans 5:3-4 says, "And not only that, but we also glory in tribulations, knowing that tribulation produces perseverance; and perseverance, character; and character, hope."

◆   ◆   ◆   ◆   ◆

Many of you will know what it means to "load the wagon." It is when you have more trials on your plate than you think you can handle. I know during the past few years my mind has been loaded almost beyond capacity.

The year 2015 brought cancer back to our home. Rhonda was diagnosed with metastatic breast cancer. The disease had returned in her bones, causing severe pain. I could not believe it — eleven years, and this mess was back, causing problems again. Most patients with this type of cancer do not live long after the diagnosis, but she amazed the doctors and nurses with her determination. Rhonda, however, was always one of the bravest and most determined persons I have ever met. She was such a great inspiration to everyone who met her. She never complained. If you asked her how she was doing, you would hear, "I am good!" She believed without a doubt that God had His hand on her and that a miracle was on the way. She was already a miracle, and such a blessing. I was proud to be a part of her beautiful life.

The days progressed, and the cancer began to take its toll on her little body. I did not want to accept that God was not sending the miracle we had been praying for. Honestly, I began to wonder why there were so many healings in the Bible — even the dead being raised! Was God not hearing our prayers? My life was sliding into the most depressing state. I was unable to function or think, as my time was spent praying continuously.

Finally, we went to see Dr. Go, and he began telling us the news we were hoping we would never hear: "There is nothing else we can do." There are no words to describe the feelings and emotions in that room. I was broken. My heart was broken, and there was no reply that could be mustered.

There was a friend of mine who lost his wife to a horrible form of cancer (not that there is any good form of cancer). He made pictures of her during her anguish, which illustrated how unbearable and horrible the disease had progressed until death finally rescued her from the agony. I told him his wife was now with God and there was no more suffering, to which he replied, "After all the praying and begging I did, there is no God! How could someone call Himself God and not liberate my wife from this atrocious disease?" I stood there speechless, wondering how he could say such a thing about God. How could anyone be led down that road?

I remembered that conversation and could easily see and feel the emotions he was enduring. There have been days when my mind would drift into the same area. These emotions are human emotions, and they can come to even the strongest Christian. They are reactions of anger and disappointment. God had these same feelings as He turned His eyes away from His Son, who, covered in our sins, was dying a horrible death on the cross for a world of lost sinners.

Rhonda said, "I want to get the funeral arrangements completed so you won't have to worry." She never wanted me to worry about anything. We went to the cemetery and the funeral home, where she told the folks exactly how she wanted things arranged. As we left, she turned to the owner of the mortuary and said, "I might see you in a few days or six months, whenever God says." Lee's eyes welled up with tears, as did mine. He said, "I believe you are one of the strongest women I have ever met." A few weeks later, my son Jay said something along the same line: "Daddy, Rhonda has truly been an inspiration to other cancer patients and other people."

A person is only capable of handling so much psychological stress. My hat is off to all those who are caretakers for their loved ones. I do not believe anyone really knows what these folks go through. I know that taking care of Rhonda was extremely difficult, just sitting by and watching as the disease deteriorated her body each day. Had it not been for God's grace, I could not, mentally or physically, have endured.

My dad passed away because of cancer, but there was something different about my Rhonda. I feel like a part of me is dying with every day that passes. We did everything together and were never apart. She was the love of my life, and I deeply miss her. I would do just about anything if I could hug her and talk to her just one more time. However, I know the day will come when I will see her again. She will be full of life, with no more pain or sickness, because she loved the Lord Jesus and she knew her destination.

People need to spend time with loved ones, because the day will come when the time runs out. The house filled with things, once a home, will seem empty and without purpose. There will be a void that you cannot fill. It is during those times you will have to rely on your faith in Jesus Christ. The psalmist said in chapter 40, verses 1-3:

I waited patiently for the Lord; And He inclined to me, And heard my cry. He also brought me up out of a horrible pit, Out of the miry clay, And set my feet upon a rock, And established my steps. He has put a new song in my mouth — Praise to our God; Many will see it and fear, And will trust in the Lord.

One must understand that, without faith in God and His promises, we have before us a grim future. David understood this at the death of his son when he said, "The child cannot come back to me, but I can someday go to him." My little Punkin' cannot come back to me, but one glorious day I can go to her.

She was a very talented decorator. She made our home so beautiful and meaningful. I can see her handiwork in every room. She adored Christmas, and I cannot explain in words what she did every year with decorations to make our home feel the joy and beauty of the wonderful season of the birth of our Lord. I told someone I hope she is not up there trying to tell Jesus how to decorate heaven.

I miss her terribly, but I want to thank God for thirty-two years of love and joy. My heart has been broken, but I look forward to the day that I will be with her again as a brother and sister in Christ, when we will both know and feel the true love that is in Jesus Christ.

I was privileged to officiate at her funeral. Many ask how I found the courage to preach my own wife's funeral. I was able to do it because she asked that I preach it and, most of all, because of the strength I received from the power of the Holy Spirit. The Spirit held me up and strengthened me, both mentally and physically, to publicly celebrate her wonderful life.

There were so many people who attended the funeral, and as each came by to speak to me, they would tell me how Rhonda had touched their lives. One young lad said, "If it had not been for Miss Rhonda, I wouldn't be alive today." She gave of herself to everyone with whom she came in contact.

◆　◆　◆　◆　◆

Please allow me to expound a moment on cancer. It is the most damnable, debilitating, devastating disease. It kills over 600,000 men, women and children every year. It does not matter who you are or where you are from, it attacks and slowly kills its victims. It not only attacks the patient, but it also attacks the whole family.

Every day, your hopes go up and down like the waves of the ocean. The doctors do everything in their power to give the patient a few more days, weeks or years to live. But sometimes the treatments only make the person sicker, and their quality of life is not one they can enjoy.

I have often wondered why we can do all of the great things we do in this world, but it seems no doctor, professor, medical expert, pharmaceutical expert, or expert on the study of the disease has a clue how to put an end to it.

Not all cancer prognoses end in death. There are many times God uses the medicines, doctors, surgeons and nurses to actually eradicate the disease and allow the patient to live out a normal life. These, of course, are considered miracles. But God doesn't always intervene. Sometimes cancer is the patient's time to go home.

CHAPTER 11

WHY BAD THINGS HAPPEN TO GOOD PEOPLE

Have you ever thought, "What is going on in my life?" I watched my little wife suffer with cancer. I have seen the pain and the agony of the chemotherapy treatments. I have stood by while she suffered the pain of bone and liver biopsies, and she never complained.

I watched, and I just could not understand how someone who was so close to Christ, a person who would give you her last cent if she thought it would help, should have to suffer the way she did. A wonderful woman who had taken care of me through my bout with this terrible disease. I was there when she waited on her sister hand and foot as she lay dying from lung cancer. I will never forget that cold January night when Rhonda went to Debbie's bedside and lovingly washed her body before the funeral home arrived to take her away.

One night in early spring we received a call from Rhonda's mother that her stepfather was dying. Rhonda, sick with cancer, went to her mother's side and spent the night until the time came for Jerry to depart this world. She gave of herself so that someone else might be comforted.

I have counseled couples whose marriages were crumbling around them like a house of cards, one loving with all their heart while the other had ideas of their own, good women and good men being torn into little pieces and having no idea why this was happening.

I have stood at the bedside of little children who were so sick that death appeared imminent. Doctors coming in and out with their long white coats and stethoscopes hanging from their necks. The child's mom, dad, and the family sitting around the dark room with tears silently streaming down their cheeks, waiting for the doctors to give them some words of encouragement.

I remember officiating at the funeral for a young man who died of suicide. He was a good kid who seemed to love life. He loved sports and enjoyed accompanying his grandfather to the games. They loved to sit around and talk about the games they had attended or watched on Saturday afternoons while downing hot dogs, chips, and Cokes. He loved doing odd jobs around the house for his mother and grandmother and anyone else who asked. On that dreadful day, as I walked into the house, the mother was broken and distraught, screaming, "Why?" The whole family was there, all wanting to hear an answer to why he would do such a terrible thing. The sheriff's sergeant and I looked on, and neither of us had an answer to the question they most wanted answered: "Why?" It wasn't long after that terrible event that the boy's grandfather died. Some may say, and I must agree, that he died from a broken heart.

My daughter once told me it seems as if bad things come in groups. I must agree; it seems when life goes into the valley, the valley seems long, dark and treacherous.

David wrote these words in the twenty-third psalm: "Yea, though I walk through the valley of the shadow of death, I will fear no evil: for thou art with me; thy rod and thy staff, they comfort me." These words have carried me through so many tragic moments. Notice the word shadow. It is only a shadow. I try to keep that in mind when I am on one of those journeys through the darkest valleys.

But let me get back to that three-letter word that seems to have no answer: why. Its Merriam Webster definition — "the cause or reason for something" — doesn't seem to assist in understanding the "why things happen" question. In response to our need to know why, the Bible says, "And we know that all things work together for good to those who love God, to those who are the called according to His purpose" (Romans 8:28). The Scripture itself may not be what we want to hear during those times we are asking why bad things happen to good people, but we need to understand the inspiration guiding Paul, the Apostle, when he wrote these beautiful words in his letter to the Christians at the church of Rome. Paul was inspired by the Holy Spirit of God. We need to understand that God lives in the past, present and future. Therefore, He knows why things happen the way they do.

Let me share an illustration. You get up one morning, and everything goes wrong. I know you have had such mornings, when you wanted to just get back under the covers and stay at home. But you keep plugging away — getting your shower, then getting dressed and ready, only to realize you'll be late to your destination. On the way, you notice the blue and red lights ahead, and as you slowly get closer, you see the twisted metal, broken glass and other debris scattered in the roadway. A terrible accident has taken place, and you see the white sheets draped over the remains of the occupants who were driving the torn and destroyed vehicles. Did you stop to think that it could have been you, had everything gone right before you left home? God kept you home and out of the ensuing accident.

Sometimes when we wonder why bad things happen to good people, we need to remember Paul's inspired words in the Scripture. God knows what is best for us, and He knows what is best for those good people when bad things happen to them.

Some blame God for the terrible things that happen. We live in a sin-cursed world. Adam and Eve lived in a perfect environment in the Garden of Eden. Sin did not exist, nor did any of the catastrophes we experience, such as earthquakes, flooding, hurricanes, and many other calamities. This is the world in which God intended for us to live.

God told Adam and Eve they could eat of any of the fruit of the garden except one tree. One day as Eve walked in the garden, she was approached by Satan, disguised as a serpent. He deceived her concerning God's order about eating of the fruit of this particular tree. After Eve's discussion with Satan, she looked at the fruit and saw that it was good. So she reached to the limb of the tree and picked the forbidden fruit and took the first bite of sin. She passed the fruit to Adam, who also partook. Because of their deeds, Adam and Eve were put out of the garden. To many, this might seem to have been a trivial issue, one that should not have carried such a harsh penalty. But because they dishonored God's command, the punishment for their evil act brought a curse on both the human race and all of creation.

We live in a sin-cursed world, and bad things are going to happen to both the good and the bad. Jesus said in John 16:33, "In the world you will have tribulation; but be of good cheer, I have overcome the world."

If we put our trust in Jesus Christ, who came to earth and paid the price for sin, then our minds should not be on the terrible things of this world but on the place Jesus has prepared for us to spend eternity.

CHAPTER 12

ANSWER YOUR CALL IN LIFE

God called me to the ministry at the young age of twenty-three. The day it happened, I was driving to Pelzer, South Carolina. It was a beautiful sunny day, and as I crossed over the old river bridge, the mist from the water falling over the dam spread across my windshield. It was is if the mist brought God into my truck, and it felt as though He was sitting in the truck with me. I knew without a doubt it was the Spirit working in my mind and heart. My chest was burning, and it was like I couldn't form any words back to Him. I was considering just asking Him to get out on the other side of the bridge.

The encounter rested heavy on my heart. I began thinking of what the acceptance of the calling would mean to me and my family. More education was the first thing that crossed my mind. Then my thinking turned to moving away from family and friends. A Scripture verse began resting heavy on my mind. Jesus said in Luke 14:26-27, "If anyone comes to Me and does not hate his father and mother, wife and children, brothers and sisters, yes, and his own life also, he cannot be My disciple. And whoever does not bear his cross and come after Me cannot be My disciple."

Hindsight is 20/20. Had I known then what is evident to me today, I would have immediately answered the call. I made the wrong choice. I decided I was not going to be a pastor under any conditions. That decision created in me a rebellious attitude toward God. The result was that my home being broken, followed by years of mental anguish.

It has been my motto to tell folks, both young and old, to be careful with their choices, because the wrong choice can haunt you for a lifetime.

My experience with colorectal cancer was life-changing, to say the least. God put me in a position where I could only trust and listen to Him. When God has something for you to do, there is no changing His will. The one whose will be changed is yours. What we human beings can't understand is, God knows what is best for us."

After my experience with cancer, I was reminded that God had called me to the ministry back in 1973. I had fought that calling for many years. Now that I was divorced, with a horrible past, I thought I could never be a minister — and especially an effective one. But the call got stronger. I decided I would reenter college and get a degree in Bible studies and would become a chaplain. "That should satisfy God," I thought. I explained to Him that I could not meet any of the qualifications to be a Baptist minister. That did not stop the gnawing inside my heart. I couldn't rest. I couldn't get comfortable in church. I was miserable.

Then it happened. One Sunday morning when the pastor had finished his sermon, I couldn't hold it back any longer. I went to the front and said, "God is calling me to preach the gospel." Jamie, our pastor, looked at me and was speechless. He knew the rules of the church, and he never said anymore about it.

A few months later we were blessed with another pastor. His name was Mike Thompson. He was a man who knew about trials and tribulations. He was bound to a wheelchair because of multiple sclerosis. He and I talked about my situation on several occasions, and I told him I was going to preach even if I had to go to another denomination. He took out his Bible and turned to 1 Timothy 3:1-7 and read:

This is a faithful saying: If a man desires the position of a bishop, he desires a good work. A bishop then must be blameless, the husband of one wife, temperate, sober-minded, of good behavior, hospitable, able to teach; not given to wine, not violent, not greedy for money, but gentle, not quarrelsome, not covetous; one who rules his own house well, having his children in submission with all reverence (for if a man does not know how to rule his own house, how will he take care of the church of God?); not a novice, lest being puffed up with pride he fall into the same condemnation as the devil. Moreover he must have a good testimony among those who are outside, lest he fall into reproach and the snare of the devil.

Then he looked me square in the eyes and said "You have only pointed out one of the requirements, what about all the others? Do you know of anyone that can say they meet all of these qualifications?" Words would not come.

A brief time later I was ordained. In only a few months I was called as senior pastor of WayCross Baptist Church. The story of the prodigal son had never been as real to me as it was that day six years ago. When the voting was over and one hundred percent of the people had voted for me to be their pastor, I knew right then that, like David, I was forgiven, and my soul had been restored.

I have a close friend who is a member of our church. He and a friend were coming home from a race in Charlotte, North Carolina, one night. They both were intoxicated. Along the interstate they lost control of the vehicle they were driving, and my friend was severely injured, paralyzed from the upper chest down. A while after the accident, he and his wife accepted Christ as Savior. He is an amazing person. Of course, he is a cantankerous ole goat, but he is still one of my best friends. I was blessed to take him to a meeting at a neighboring church where he was the main speaker. He worried the whole way over that he would not know what to say. He almost wished he had not accepted the invitation. He brought a beautiful and blessed message, and when he ended his talk, six men accepted Christ. Had there been no tragedy and his life not been changed, we can only think about what might have happened to those six men. Maybe God would have sent someone else. Or was it God's will for my buddy to be hurt in order to be there to lead those men into the kingdom?

There is another man, Butch, whose life was changed by God. He has a beautiful wife and family. He is a truck driver and has a wonderful personality. He has more stories about life on the highway than the state troopers. He had strayed from God and left the fellowship of the church. He allowed Satan to lead him into a life of addiction. It was a horrible experience for him. To this day he continues to fight the guilt of his past.

When it comes to our pasts, many of us are like Butch. It is easy to be a Monday-morning quarterback. It is easy to look back and see what we should or should not have done, but there is no fix for the past. The past is exactly that: the past. For the Christian, your past is Satan's favorite subject. He loves to keep bringing it up in your mind just at that moment when memories of your past are the last thing you need. It is his diabolic plan to torment and continually accuse you.

I believe Paul had it down pat when he wrote these words in Philippians 3:12-14:

> Not that I have already attained, or am already perfected; but I press on, that I may lay hold of that for which Christ Jesus has also laid hold of me. Brethren, I do not count myself to have apprehended; but one thing I do, forgetting those things which are behind and reaching forward to those things which are ahead, I

press toward the goal for the prize of the upward call of God in Christ Jesus.

Butch had a touch from God. He returned to church, rededicated his life, and now is our youth minister and a deacon, and he fills the pulpit while I am away. His personality hasn't changed; he is still as jolly and loving as can be. He is touching the lives of people on his job and the young people he leads at our church. He has answered the call!

CHAPTER 13

FINDING YOUR PURPOSE

Peter wrote in 1 Peter 4:10-11:

As each one has received a gift, minister it to one another, as good stewards of the manifold grace of God. If anyone speaks, let him speak as the oracles of God. If anyone ministers, let him do it as with the ability which God supplies, that in all things God may be glorified through Jesus Christ, to whom belong the glory and the dominion forever and ever. Amen.

Charles Kingsley, writing in Bits & Pieces (Dec. 9, 1993), says, "We function as though comfort and luxury were the chief requirements of life, when all that we need to make us happy is something to be enthusiastic about."

Our purpose is a calling. God calls many people to different vocations so that they can be ministers to help, support, and guide those under their care. I have met many people: superintendents, nurses, doctors, lawyers, mechanics, custodians, plumbers, electricians, and many more, who believe their position in life was appointed by God. They use their positions to minister to people's needs. Because of their dedication each day, they are making a difference in the world and in individuals' lives. These professionals go out each day with a purpose, and they pursue that purpose with a persistent passion.

God saw a need to place each of us here for a certain purpose. Many of us have spent the best part of our lives trying to find that purpose. The purpose you are looking for will be a blessing to people in your life, every day. Believe me: You have a purpose. It is something you totally enjoy doing, and not only that, the fulfillment you experience will be overflowing.

I had a teacher in high school, Miss Garrett. Not only was she a great teacher, she was a wonderful person, as well. Her purpose was to educate the students under her care, and that she did with splendor and perfection. She would go the extra mile to make sure her students mastered the subject matter. I have never forgotten the times she would sit and talk to me about how important my future was and how I would be a blessing to people. It wasn't only me she spent that extra time with; there were many others through the years who sat with her and listened as she cheered them on toward a successful future.

There was a dentist in our community, a wonderful Christian lady. She was not only a great dentist, but also a great lady. She would spend time every summer in some foreign country or another doing free dental work for the less fortunate. She felt it was her purpose to help those people who, without her sacrifice, would never have the dental care they needed.

Paul wrote to Timothy about God's purpose in their lives: "[God] has saved us and called us with a holy calling, not according to our works, but according to His own purpose and grace which was given to us in Christ Jesus before time began" (2 Timothy 1:9).

God has called His children to fulfill a certain purpose in life. There was a great man in the Bible, his name was Moses. He, like many others, was called for a certain purpose. His purpose was to lead the people of Israel to the promised land. He doubted his abilities and made excuses in an attempt to be freed from God's calling. God never let Moses back down, and He gave him the tools he needed to free the people from their slavery in Egypt.

When you finally realize your purpose in life, you will find overwhelming joy. Life is more fulfilling when you find that you have a valuable place in society and a motivation for living a happy and productive life that your family and friends will appreciate and remember.

CHAPTER 14

LESSONS DURING THE STORMS

I know of a young man who lived in Charleston, South Carolina. He was working for the Navy as a private engineer. He loved to hunt and had an ole hunting dog that stayed by his side all the time. It was during his time in Charleston that Hurricane Hugo made landfall dead center on the historic city. Bill had never seen a hurricane in action, so he decided he and his dog would ride this one out.

The night the storm struck, with winds well over 150 miles per hour, there was Bill and his trusted hunting dog by his side in the house. The lights began to flicker, and the house began to squeak and crack as the howling, deafening wind become stronger and stronger. They could hear the trees begin to crack and fall, some touching the house and sliding down the outside walls of the house to find their resting place at the foundation. It was beginning to be more than he had bargained for, and he knew he and the dog were going to need a safer place than the bedroom if they expected to survive. The two of them went downstairs, dragging a very large mattress, as fast as a human and a dog could move. They charged the old cast iron bathtub at full speed, getting into the tub and pulling the mattress over them.

They were experiencing the frontal approach of the storm, not realizing there would be a lull as the eye of the hurricane passed over them; then, what they had just experienced with so much fear was about to come at them again.

The wonderful thing was that they survived the storm. Both walked out of the house without a scratch, but the memory of that horrific night still lives on in Bill's mind. When he tells the story of that night and his decision to ride out the storm, you can still see the grip that fear had on him.

There are some storms in life for which we are not a party to the decision about our personal involvement. We didn't just sit down one day and say, "I am going to sit this one out just to see how big it is." We didn't go out and buy batteries, bread, milk, and peanut butter. These storms come without warning. There are no alarms blaring, no police officers coming to warn us to get out of its way.

These are the storms of life, and no one is exempt from their assault. They come in different forms; no two are alike. It may be the loss of a loved one, a financial disaster, debilitating disease, divorce, or perhaps a tragic accident. We never know what to expect; all we know is, there is a storm coming.

The disciples of Jesus encountered such a storm one night. We find the story in Mark 4:35-41:

> On the same day, when evening had come, He said to them, "Let us cross over to the other side." Now when they had left the multitude, they took Him along in the boat as He was. And other little boats were also with Him. And a great windstorm arose, and the waves beat into the boat, so that it was already filling. But He was in the stern, asleep on a pillow. And they awoke Him and said to Him, "Teacher, do You not care that we are perishing?" Then He arose and rebuked the wind, and said to the sea, "Peace, be still!" And the wind ceased and there was a great calm. But He said to them, "Why are you so fearful? How is it that you have no faith?" And they feared exceedingly, and said

to one another, "Who can this be, that even the wind and the sea obey Him!"

I and many others have learned when you find yourself in the middle of a storm, you must turn to the Man who can still the waters. He can calm any storm that may come your way if only you have the faith to believe, without a doubt, that He can do so.

James 1:6 gives us these words about doubting: "But let him ask in faith, with no doubting, for he who doubts is like a wave of the sea driven and tossed by the wind."

If we want His help in troubled times, we must trust Him with all our heart and have faith that He can deliver on His promises. Some may say that is hard to do. Many of you will go into your office or classroom and sit right down in your chair and begin your day. How many of you have ever walked around that chair, picked it up to make sure all the screws are tight and in the right place, or maybe just pushed it up and down to make sure it is steady enough to carry your weight? I would say no one does that. I notice people coming into the auditorium on Sundays, and no one checks any of the pews before sitting down on them. If we can trust an office chair, a classroom chair, or a church pew, then we must have faith that all of them will support us. It is amazing how we have faith in things without even giving it a thought, but with God we doubt.

Sometimes the problem is when something serious comes along. This is the real test of faith! All are human and all have doubts and questions during these times. We read in the Bible that nothing is impossible for God. We try to concentrate on those words as hard as we can. We want to believe them without the doubt.

When things are seriously bad, doubt does move into place in our minds. We pray and we repeat these words over and over, with no results. It is like God is not listening, or we think maybe He just doesn't care or that there are some things that God can't do.

Let me give you some relief here. You are not alone with these thoughts. Satan loves to inject his words of doubt into your mind. I have known people who turned against God because they thought He didn't care about their dilemma. Some have lost belief in their Creator. So many lives have been ruined because they allowed their unbelief to overcome their faith in the living God.

I know it is hard when it seems God is off doing something else more important than attending to our need. One thing to keep in mind during these times is Psalm 107:29-39:

> *He calms the storm, So that its waves are still. Then they are glad because they are quiet; So He guides them to their desired haven. Oh, that men would give thanks to the Lord for His goodness, And for His wonderful works to the children of men! Let them exalt Him also in the assembly of the people, And praise Him in the company of the elders. He turns rivers into a wilderness, And the watersprings into dry ground; A fruitful land into barrenness, For the wickedness of those who dwell in it. He turns a wilderness into pools of water, And dry land into watersprings. There He makes the hungry dwell, That they may establish a city for a dwelling place, And sow fields and plant vineyards, That they may yield a fruitful harvest. He also blesses them, and they multiply greatly; And He does not let their cattle decrease. When they are diminished and brought low Through oppression, affliction and sorrow ....*

Peter's faith failed him. For a brief and terrifying moment, he took his eyes off the Lord, and he began to go beneath the water. When Peter was weak and sinking, Jesus reached down, picked him up, and put him back in the boat.

When your storm rages and you begin to question God's presence or God's concern for your circumstances, just reach up and take Him by the hand. He will get you back in the boat and out of the storm. Just trust Him.

CHAPTER 15

PRACTICING SELF-CONTROL

The Scriptures warn us if we don't have self-control, then we will be a slave to whatever controls us. Take eating, for an example: If you can't control yourself at the buffet, you will gain weight. The same is true with spending money; if you can't control your spending, you will not have anything left to spend.

In today's society, self-control has fallen by the wayside. Take a ride around the city sometimes. You will see road rage, people shaking their fist, or putting their finger into your line of sight. They have no self-control. Marriages are falling apart every day, and robberies and murders are a daily occurrence for the same reason: lack of self-control.

"For the grace of God has appeared that offers salvation to all people. It teaches us to say 'No' to ungodliness and worldly passions, and to live self-controlled, upright and godly lives in this present age" (Titus 2:11-12, NIV).

Proverbs 3:21 tells us, "My son, let them not depart from your eyes — Keep sound wisdom and discretion."

On a cool spring morning, there was a young boy sitting in a chair outside his house. Beside him was an old dog that went everywhere the youngster decided to go. On the other side was a beat-up and battered looking lawnmower with a handwritten sign that said "For sale." After an hour or so had passed, the boy noticed a man wearing a suit and tie strolling down the sidewalk with an umbrella in one hand a Bible in the other. The man stopped and, with interest in his eyes, asked the boy, "Does it run?" The boy said, "Yes, it runs like a charm." So the man laid his umbrella and Bible aside and began to pull the rope furiously in an attempt to bring the mower to life, with no success. He said to the boy, "This thing will not start as you said it would." The boy said, "You gotta cuss it, mister," to which the man replied, "I have been a Baptist preacher for many years, and I am not going back to my old ways."

That is what Solomon was saying to us when he penned the Scripture above. It takes self-control to keep old habits from returning. It is not an easy task, but with God's help we can control our actions.

I have been playing the game of golf since the age of ten. I would play with my dad and his friends, and of course they all thought they should be on the professional tour. Some days they would have me in some of the most awkward positions, trying to teach me how to hit the ball straight. It is surprising I didn't break or strain something that would have ruined me for life.

The game of golf is a great teacher. You may play in a foursome, but you play the game against yourself. It is one of the few games that requires your constant attention. Concentration is necessary on each shot; if you lose your focus, the ball will end up in a troubled spot. If you let one bad shot get into your head, it can ruin the rest of your round. Playing golf is a lot like life: You play it one shot at the time; some shots are good, and some not so good.

I have played with some interesting people. Once there was a guy who would throw his club each time he made a bad shot. When his ball went into the woods or the water, we would immediately take shelter. He would then look around with disgust on his face and then begin the search for both the club and the ball. His actions would be repeated several times as we played the rest of the course. He could not control his emotions.

There was another occasion when I was playing with one of the regular groups and one of guys who had not being playing so well hit his ball into the lake. After a blast of cursing, he took his clubs off the cart, and I thought he is going to throw them in the lake. But instead, he put the strap over his shoulder and walked away, grumbling, never to play the game again.

There are people who respond to their mistakes in life with the same behavior, going into fits of rage because something at home or work, or sometimes even at church, did not go their way.

A hot temper is a strange thing. People who easily lose control of their temper usually say the wrong things and hurt someone or create a dilemma out of something they are doing.

My dad had a flaring temper on occasion. He had purchased a new Chevrolet truck. It was green and white and had the nicest hub caps, along with all the latest accessories. One beautiful summer day, the sun was shining bright, reflecting off the tailgate of Dad's new pickup, parked under the grain barn. He had gotten himself into a rage about something Mother said and went tearing out of the house, down the steps and into the grain barn. We knew one of his famous tantrums was in its preliminary stages. Mother walked to the door, as my brother and I peeped out from behind her to see what was going to happen.

He cranked his pride and joy, slammed it into reverse and attempted to blast out of the barn. And then it happened. There was a large bolt he had installed into the block so he could add doors to the barn. The bolt caught the passenger side door and opened that new, beautiful, shiny green-painted metal like an old can opener. His rage worsened, so then he started jerking the vehicle back and forth until it shot halfway down the driveway. My brother and I looked up at our mother, and she had the most beautiful smile on her face. I still wonder to this day what she was smiling about.

There are folks you and I have had the pleasure of working with who use their temperaments as a means for bulling their employees or coworkers. You know the ones I am speaking about: They are the folks who will say, "You don't want to make me mad." You arrive at the workplace, and everyone starts passing along the warning: He or she is in one of their moods today, outraged about something, so stay out of their way! These are the folks most people just want to evade. If they are leaders of the business, the dilemma becomes more challenging. It not only affects a small number of employees, but the entire workforce. Genuine leadership does not incorporate this type of behavior. Proverbs 29:11 describes anger very well: "A fool vents all his feelings, but a wise man holds them back."

Controlling one's speech is a challenge. James said, "By our speech we can ruin the world, turn harmony to chaos, throw mud on a reputation, send the whole world up in smoke and go up in smoke with it, smoke right from the pit of hell" (James 3:6, MSG).

The key is to put your brain in gear before engaging your tongue. Always remember that God gave us two ears and only one tongue. He must have had a good reason for that decision.

CHAPTER 16

WHY WAS I BORN?

Have you ever asked yourself that question? I know the question has crossed my mind on certain occasions. Many have sensed there was simply no objective for their life. Many believe their lives represent little in the grand scheme of events, and because of this some have lived humdrum lives and never sought to understand their purpose on God's green earth.

We each have a purpose. We are not here on a whim or by some accident. Do you recognize that God knew you well before the day you were born? Your precise birth date was set prior to the earth's creation. I realize this statement is extraordinary, but don't be dismayed. God reveals this truth to us in Jeremiah 1:5: "Before I formed you in the womb I knew you." God not only knew Jeremiah before he developed in his mother's womb, He also knew what the purpose of Jeremiah's life would be.

Most of us are not a priest, preacher, prophet or an apostle, but I feel the opening part of this verse relates to all of us. God says, "Before I formed you in the womb I knew you." He further says, "Before you were born I sanctified you." He has established us separately. He has made us unique.

Look around you. There are no two people exactly alike, not even identical twins. There are people of distinct colors and shapes. Some are tall, some are short. Some have hair on their heads, and there are those who do not. Everyone is different.

There are some who wished they had never been born. There was a man in the Old Testament, Job, who was extremely rich, with many animals and much gold. He was also rich in family, with ten children. One day he lost everything except his life and his wife (who, by the way, told him to curse God and die). His response to his situation was a human one. He was so distraught that his life was in shambles that he deplored the day he was born:

> *After this Job opened his mouth and cursed the day of his birth. And Job spoke, and said: "May the day perish on which I was born, And the night in which it was said, 'A male child is conceived.' May that day be darkness; May God above not seek it, Nor the light shine upon it." (Job 3:1-4)*

The good news in this story is that God gave him a fresh start in life. By the grace of God, all he had lost was restored as it was before. The significance of this story is this: Once you get beaten and are down and out, you climb out of the chasm you have plummeted into and start once again.

The first thing we need to do is find our proper place in life and get in alignment with God's remarkable plan for our lives. Remember: He is the one who placed us here, and for a certain reason. If we are out of position with God's will for our life, failure can be expected.

No one should regret being here on this earth or the reason they were placed in their current position. According to a widely referenced story, Martin Luther King Jr., speaking to a group of junior high school students six months before he was assassinated, said, "If it falls your lot to be a street sweeper, sweep streets like Michelangelo painted pictures, sweep streets like Beethoven composed music, ... like Shakespeare wrote poetry. Sweep streets so well that all the hosts of heaven and earth will have to pause and say: Here lived a great street sweeper who [did] his job well."

Yes, your purpose might be to work as a street sweeper or a sanitation worker. You might be a carpenter or an airline pilot, but do it well, because that is why God placed you here. He has His motives for our assignment, and it would be to our advantage to follow His blueprint for our lives. Proverbs 3:6 says, "In all your ways submit to him, and he will make your paths straight" (NIV).

You can minister to people regardless of where you spend your precious time. You can be a shining light for Christ while mopping in the school cafeteria or sitting behind the Oval Office desk in Washington. Every person in this world — past, present and future — has contributed something great or something small, something good or something evil. That is the reason you and I were born.

CHAPTER 17

HAVE A GOOD TIME

Everyone should have a hobby. A hobby is good for a person's health (unless you want to race motorcycles or climb Mount Everest). I have seen some interesting hobbies during my life.

I met a man who collected old cars. He owned a factory that made parts for the textile business and was quite wealthy. He was always on the lookout for a peculiar old car that he could add to his collection.

I have seen people collect anything from bottles to antiques. I am fascinated every time I turn on the TV to watch a show called *American Pickers*. It amazes me how much people collect and how they sometimes let it get out of hand.

My hobby is golf, because it can make you so mad that you forget everything you might have been worried about before you teed off. The greatest thing about golf is the people you play with. You can make so many friends on the course. It can get expensive if you try to "buy the game." Some of the people buy the latest balls and equipment, hoping for more distance and accuracy.

Funny things happen on the course. We had a group that played together for well over twenty years. There were some characters in the group, some you had to keep your eyes on because, under pressure, they tended to drop an extra ball when they lost theirs.

One beautiful Saturday we were ready to play, standing around and loosening up and spinning yarn. The foursome ahead of us began, and we watched as they drove their carts down the manicured green fairway lined with tall southern oaks. One of the guys in our foursome, who was walking instead of riding, was on the tee box, ready to hit when the first group cleared. Two of the others in our group forgot something in their car and went to fetch it. The guy who was walking hit his ball, and I observed as it found its way to trees. There was banging and knocking as the ball bounced from tree to tree. He started walking at once, at a fast pace, to the area where his ball had flown.

When the others returned, I was standing on the box, looking down the fairway. They asked where our fourth was, and I explained what had happened while they were gone. We then hit some nice-looking drives, and the balls rolled to a stop in the middle of the fairway. The other guy was already standing on the green with his ball in his pocket. When we arrived, he quickly let us know he had already birded the hole, so we had no worries. I set out to count his strokes, and they did not add up to a birdie. Thank goodness one of our other playing partners putted in a long birdie, so there was no need to count the first guy's score.

I believe anyone who will be untruthful on the golf course will do the same away from the course. You can discover a person's integrity on the golf course clearer and quicker than anywhere else. Solomon said, in Proverbs 12:22, "Lying lips are an abomination to the Lord, but those who deal truthfully are His delight."

It is so much easier to tell the truth than to tell a lie. My dad always told me the truth would support itself while a lie would need constant propping up. The truth is easy — because it is the truth and it doesn't change.

CHAPTER 18

FAMILY FUNNIES

"A merry heart does good, like medicine." (Proverbs 17:22)

Family members can be the most entertaining people in the world. You never know what they will say or do.

I had one of the greatest grandmothers. She was one of the most charismatic women I have ever met. She was one of the best cooks that ever lived, with a personality that would shine no matter the circumstances. She loved to garden, and did so until in her late eighties. You could find her during the hottest parts of the day, hoeing and weeding her exceptionally large garden.

She loved chickens and had a lot of them. My brother and I had received BB guns under the Christmas tree. One winter morning we decided to declare war on the chicken yard. We crept up on the chickens and settled behind a giant cedar tree in Grannie's backyard. We thought we were snipers, and we began firing at the backside of the hens and the big ole Road Island Red rooster, who thought he was the baddest rooster this side of the Mississippi.

We thought no one was watching as our attack was well under way. All of a sudden there was a voice from the other side of the tree. The voice was stern, with more force than you can imagine. Grannie had formed a surprise attack on us and, without notice, took our guns and proceeded to apply a dose of hickory tea to our backsides. We never again harassed or shot at those chickens.

We attended the reunion for Grannie's family. It was a large family with thirteen children. It was held at the park under one of the shelters the city provided. It was a beautiful Sunday afternoon, and a crowd of people were in attendance. We had a great time socializing with family members talking about old times.

My grandmother had false teeth, which she refused to wear while eating. She would wrap them in a napkin and place them in her purse. This time she placed them on the table beside her plate. When cleanup time came, Grannie's choppers ended up in the trash. She didn't miss them until she was home. She called me and said, "I believe I have lost my teeth." I said, "Grannie, if you would keep them in your mouth, you wouldn't have lost them."

My brother and I returned to the park with our dump truck and placed the trash from every single garbage receptacle on the truck. We then went home and dumped it beside her house. There we were, pilfering through a dump-truck load of stinking garbage, looking for Grannie's teeth. After about four hours, the teeth were found. She was so happy to have her teeth back, and my brother and I were standing there drenched in stinking trash. Moral to this story: Keep your teeth in your mouth, where they belong.

Grannie was very superstitious. When I became a grown man, she "required" me to come to her house every New Year's morning to ensure a successful season with her chickens.

Once my Grandfather Coot and Grannie were in a serious discussion about when the corn crop would be planted on the farm. She told him if he didn't plant in the proper signs, he would have a terrible harvest. He looked at her for a moment and then tilted his Stetson fedora back on his head, took a deep drag off of his Camel cigarette, and said, "Emma, you can plant your garden whenever you want after I plow it for you. But as for the corn, I am not planting it in any signs. I am planting it in the ground." He had an abundant crop that year. I never remember Grannie mentioning the astrological signs to Pha-Pha again.

One of my grandmother's brothers was always doing something that would split your sides with laughter. On a trip to the beach, he was sitting under his umbrella watching the waves come and go and, of course, the people who were strolling up and down the beach. He noticed the seagulls landing around him, searching for food someone might have left behind. He found the birds to be interesting.

After observing the birds for a while, he decided to return to the condo and get a box of Cheerios his wife had brought for the family to eat. He grabbed the cereal, which had not been opened and returned to the beach. He settled back into his chair under the umbrella and began looking for the birds as he opened the box of breakfast cereal. He saw that the birds were a short distance down the beach. He got up and began to walk toward the birds. His intention was to bring the birds closer, so he took the bag out of the box and threw the contents into the air.

He never considered how many seagulls hang out at the beach. As the cereal flew into the air, a multitude of gulls swarmed like flies around his head. Panic set in and he began to flee, not realizing the Cheerios were still falling from the bag as he ran. The flock of birds, which had grown in number, chased him down the beach as the people on the beach began to laugh profusely. He ran to the condo without stopping, birds flying and squawking around his head. What he didn't realize was his whole family was on the balcony laughing while he did his best to escape the birds. To this day, the mention of this incident still brings laughter to the whole family.

My wife ordered some stones to add to our landscaping. She called the big-box store and told them she wanted twenty bags of river stone and asked if they would deliver. The person on the phone asked what color she needed, and she responded that mixed colors would be fine. The clerk returned to phone and said, "We are out of the stones you want, but one of our other stores located in another city has them in stock."

Rhonda wanted the stones shipped to our house right away. The clerk informed her there would be an extra charge for the delivery. And not only would there be a charge, but delivery wouldn't be until the next day. Reluctantly, she told them to bring them the following day.

The next day, this large blue and white truck arrived at our driveway. My brother and I were outside my shop when the driver came walking down the drive with papers in hand. He said he had some special stones someone at this address wanted delivered quick. I told him he was at the right address, so he went back to the truck. Cooter and I figured he was going to get the forklift off the back of the truck, but no, he comes back carrying a box. He said whoever ordered these never considered the cost of delivery from another city. The delivery cost was more than the stones he was holding in his hands. He set the little box down, and inside were these decorative little black stones in small plastic containers.

We all started laughing, because she was expecting a large load of stones. The driver left, and Cooter and I could not wait to get Rhonda out there to see what she had ordered. The look on her beautiful little face was priceless. She said, "What am I supposed to do with those little ole things?" Cooter said, "Well, sister-in-law, I don't believe they will be too heavy to carry."

While on vacation at Hilton Head Island, my brother and I decided to play one of the ocean courses at Sea Pines and take our wives along to drive the golf carts. We had played a few holes when my ball rolled up beside a ferocious-looking ten-foot alligator sunning beside one of the attractive ponds guarding the putting green. My decision was to drop another ball and let the gator have the first one.

Rhonda said, "You are not losing a stroke over that big ugly thing." I told her it wasn't worth losing life or limb messing with the big guy with the big teeth. Before I knew it, she had found some stones and began bouncing them off the gator's head. I couldn't believe it, but he wasn't in the mood to run her down and bite off her leg (or some other atrocious response to the stones bouncing off his head). He slowly raised himself up, looking directly at Rhonda. This is not going to be good, I thought. But he just walked slowly over to the pond and slithered into the calm water and swam to the other side. Even that big ugly dangerous reptile found out how annoying my wife can be if she sets her mind to it.

Being in the National Guard was a wonderful experience. You can get into some of the most interesting things while serving your state and being a part of the United States Army. The National Guard unit I was assigned to traveled to Fort Gordon in Georgia to do annual weapons qualifying.

We drove directly to the firing range, where we were to qualify in the daylight and then take part in a nighttime firing exercise.

Every range in the army has a range boss. These fellows are well trained and expect everyone to work together and follow their orders so that everyone is safe. We were on the firing line, waiting for the tower to give the all-clear to begin firing at the targets downrange. The boss in the tower said the range was clear and to commence firing. Just as soon as he said that, a beautiful southern white tail deer walked onto the range, stopping and foraging on some grass around the target pits.

The boss tried to stop the inevitable, screaming "Cease fire!" at the top of his voice. Needless to say, one hundred guardsmen opened up on the deer, using M-16s on automatic fire with twenty-round clips. The deer broke into a full run right in front of the targets. It ran the distance and was never struck by a single bullet. We were all laughing until the range boss began chastising us (with some of the choicest words) for continuing to fire after the ceasefire order was given. He went on for several minutes, and the language continued to get worse.

That night we reported to the range for the night fire. You could barely see the targets, but you could clearly see the two large beaming red lights that were situated left and right downrange. Firing outside the red lights was prohibited. The boss gave a long lecture about safety on the range and then reminded us of the incident that occurred during day qualifying. You could tell by the tone of his voice he was in no mood for any more horseplay.

We descended into the fox holes designed for our safety and for better gun control. The boss gave the all-clear. Those two red lights were immediately shot out. He called our commanding officer to the tower and removed the entire company from the range. The boss had range rage.

All of it seemed to be just innocent fun at the time, but our actions did not help us confirm our ability to be qualified on our weapons. No one ever thought we could be in a real conflict in some foreign country in the future.

Colossians 3:23 says, "And whatever you do, do it heartily, as to the Lord and not to men."

CHAPTER 19

UNDER GOD'S PROTECTION

My National Guard company was deep in the forest on a training mission. All the vehicles were parked strategically, and tents were set up for sleeping quarters. The guys who set up the command tent was so proud of the job they had done. They boasted, "It will take a tornado to knock that one down."

Later on, in the evening, a group of us were sitting in the back of a large, drab olive green truck, playing poker, using bullets for chips. As we played, laughed and told jokes, there was an eerie quietness outside. All the deep-woods sounds seemed to have stopped. Then we heard an unusual noise coming through the trees. Tony, one of our fellow guardsmen, said, "That sounds like a freight train."

Then the wind began to blow something terrible. Someone threw the door open as the truck began to rock. I thought the wind was going to turn the vehicle over, but, instead, it was picked up and turned around, pointing in the opposite direction. One of the guys had made his bed in a trailer that we could now see from our new position. As the trailer rocked and spun around, he came out, putting his boots on in midair. We didn't see that guy again until the next weekend drill.

The large command tent that would withstand a tornado was a sight to see. The lightning was flashing and illuminating the area, so the sight of tent was clearly visible. It was like watching a slide show, only live. The sides were flapping uncontrollably while the rained poured. You could clearly see the guys who chose to sleep there in their cots, zipped up in their sleeping bags. Some were trying to loosen themselves from the sleeping bags, but with the wind gusting so hard and the sides flailing, any movement under the tent was an impossible task.

All of a sudden, the tent flew straight up, and the timbers holding it up went with it, and all of it came crashing down. We were in awe of the spectacle that was before our eyes. We jumped from the truck and ran to the tent because there were soldiers under the rubble. We were blessed that night; only one man was transported to the hospital, but later released.

I will never forget the night a tornado passed through our camp. I still remember how peaceful it was afterwards. There was an unbelievable silence in the camp as some began to walk around assessing the damage.

There was a man we called Wig who was asleep in the cab of the truck we were in. He slowly rolled down the window and said the most profound thing: "Is that tornado-proof tent still standing?"

God protected over a hundred soldiers that night. I am not sure how many thanked Him the next morning, but He had definitely showered us with a blessing. Most of us were young and thought we could conquer the world, if necessary. There was no one crying or complaining, just a group of young men who were delighted they were still alive. Young people never seem to be concerned about danger, even when it is life-threatening. It reminds me of a storm recorded in Luke 8:23-25:

> *But as they sailed He fell asleep. And a windstorm came down on the lake, and they were filling with water, and were in jeopardy. And they came to Him and awoke Him, saying, "Master, Master, we are perishing!" Then He arose and rebuked the wind and the*

raging of the water. And they ceased, and there was a calm. But He said to them, "Where is your faith?" And they were afraid, and marveled, saying to one another, "Who can this be? For He commands even the winds and water, and they obey Him!"

CHAPTER 20

MAKE HOME THE PLACE YOUR HEART IS

Home is a wonderful place, a safe haven against the threats of this world. It is the place where we can sit down with people we trust. Home represents bygone times. Home is not just a house, nor just a place to hang your hat.

Jesus saw the need for a person to have a home when He instructed John to take His mother home with him.

Home has been the subject of many songs, both Christian and secular. Remember the song "I'll Be Home for Christmas"? A part of the lyrics says, "If only in my heart."

There is one thing people never forget, and that is the home they were raised in. Even if the old house has been demolished, the memories are still held dear. That home, that house, played an important part in who they are today.

My dad took me on ride through the country one lazy Saturday. As we were driving along the narrow country road, he steered the truck over on to the shoulder of the road. We got out of the truck and began to walk through the trees. I said, "Where are we going, Daddy?" He told me he had a special surprise for me.

A few yards into the trees were the remains of an old house. It had been beaten down by the elements, and it was clear no one had tried to maintain it for years. The roof had fallen in, and trees and bushes were growing through the debris. The old faded front door was leaning, and only one rusty hinge was saving it from falling to the leaf-covered ground below. It was apparent this old house was nearing the end of its existence.

Daddy's eyes surveyed the picture before him. He didn't say anything for a while as I wandered around the site seeing what else may have survived. There were old jars and few plowshares lying around under the leaves. An old well was covered by a large piece of concrete, saplings growing from beneath it.

While I was exploring, Daddy came to where I was and said, "Son, I was born in this ole house." You could tell from the expression on his face that the place held a special place in his heart. It was his home for a brief time in his life. It was the place he began his life. It was not a place where the rich and famous lived and thrived; it was the house of a share-cropper working for half the harvest. It was here that my grandparents began their family and worked and saved so they could someday buy their own farm.

The house my brother and I were raised in still stands. My son Jay resides in the house that was once home to me. When I go there, each room holds a special memory for me. The back bedroom was Mother and Daddy's for a while, until Cooter and I were moved into the room. It was in this bedroom my dad would apply the leather to our backsides when we got in trouble — which for me was quite often.

The living room was where the Christmas tree was always placed. Mother would decorate the cedar trees that Daddy provided over the years. It was to that tree we would dash on Christmas morning to see what the old bearded man in red had left for two fine boys. I can still see the red and gray Lionel engine pulling its cars around the track, traveling under the bridge and past the depot. It had smoke billowing out the top, and the sound of the whistle blowing made a little boy feel like he was driving a real train down the track.

I can clearly remember the kitchen, where the family would sit down together and eat some of the finest food you ever tasted in your life. My mother was one of the greatest cooks I have ever known. She could make anything, and the smell of her cooking would fill the house with an aroma that would tease you unmercifully until she placed it on the table to be eaten.

My grandmother's house was well over a hundred years old. There was a Warm Morning coal heater in the family room. It was black in color, but as it grew hot from the coal fire, the steel sides would transform to red and orange like the sun on sizzling summer day. The heat would penetrate into your bones and warm you up from a frosty winter day. Our family spent hours around that heater, enjoying each other's company, eating oyster stew and drinking tea mixed with Pepsi-Cola.

At Christmas, she would have the fireplace in the living room fired up. The wood would crackle and pop, causing sparks to go up the chimney. Oh, the times we had around that fireplace! She would always fetch her own cedar tree and decorate it with ornaments and lights that bubbled when they heated up. Angel hair, as she called it, was wrapped all around the tree, which was topped off with glistening icicles hanging from every limb and a beautiful star at the very top.

On one summer day in the cool of the morning, I was riding on the Farmall Super-A tractor with my granddad. It was a treat when he sat me down on the battery box, on a pillow, right in front of him. I would ride for hours while he planted the corn crop.

He was planting the field adjacent to our house, and when we turned to plant another row, my other grandfather was pulling into our driveway. I asked Pha-Pha if I could get off and go see Papa J.D. He stopped the tractor, and I jumped off and ran as fast as my little legs would take me to the house. Mother had made some lemonade for all of us. As we were enjoying the lemonade and having an enjoyable time with each other, all of a sudden my mother screamed at the top of her lungs. My Grandfather Coot had turned the tractor over on himself. It was a horrible site for a four-year-old.

He died a few days later, and his remains were placed in the living room of Grannie's house for visitation and the wake. I was small, but I still remember the sadness that filled the room that had brought so much happiness to so many family members. My grandparents' home was just not the same anymore. I loved him so much, and to this day I still think about him.

Everyone remembers the home they were raised in. Homes hold some of the most precious memories a person possesses. However, these are brick-and-mortar buildings we hold dear. Our real house is made of dirt and clay and is referred to in the Scripture as a tent or temple:

> But the Jews were upset. They asked, "What credentials can you present to justify this?" Jesus answered, "Tear down this Temple and in three days I'll put it back together." They were indignant: "It took forty-six years to build this Temple, and you're going to rebuild it in three days?" But Jesus was talking about his body as the Temple. Later, after he was raised from the dead, his disciples remembered he had said this. They then put two and two together and believed both what was written in Scripture and what Jesus had said. (John 2:18-22, MSG)

He told His disciples He was going away to prepare a place for those who believe. John 14:2-3 gives to each of us promise: "In My Father's house are many mansions; if it were not so, I would have told you. I go to prepare a place for you. And if I go and prepare a place for you, I will come again and receive you to Myself; that where I am, there you may be also."

Our bodies are a temporary vessel for our soul. These temples, or tents, get older and older every day we live here on earth. Each day, we move a little closer to death and our departure from these bodies. Parts begin to fail. You can't see like you used to. You reach the point that your brain begins to require more than the body can deliver. (Sometimes I think that is the worst part of getting older; you design a project around the house or on the farm, only to discover the body cannot meet the brain's demand.)

Second Corinthians 5:1 says, "For we know that if our earthly house, this tent, is destroyed, we have a building from God, a house not made with hands, eternal in the heavens."

That is the home we are looking for. It is the home that Jesus promised. He promised that everybody who believes he is the Son of God, and believes he died on that old, rugged cross at a place called Calvary, and on the third day rose victoriously from the tomb, will be invited to live in His kingdom for eternity. This home is our real and final home, a place where the body will never age nor experience sickness again. There will be no more death. We will have reached our destination. We will have made it home.

Heaven is such a wonderful and exciting place to think about. It is place where we will serve the one and only God we have believed in for so long. It will be an endless time of rejoicing and walking along streets of gold. The best thing about it is that we can sit down with Jesus and talk with Him face to face. And not only Jesus, but the great heroes of the Bible we have read so much about. Think about that for a moment; you can sit down and talk with Moses about the crossing of the Red Sea, or Joshua about the excitement of the walls of Jericho falling. All the writers of the sixty-six books of the Bible will be there. You can discuss the books they were inspired to write. It will be a place you can feel the love of God throughout eternity.

Sadness also comes to my heart when I think about heaven, because so many will miss the opportunity to be there. Jesus was quite clear about this when He said, in Matthew 7:13-14: "Enter by the narrow gate; for wide is the gate and broad is the way that leads to destruction, and there are many who go in by it. Because narrow is the gate and difficult is the way which leads to life, and there are few who find it."

The Message translates the same text in a more understanding way: "Don't look for shortcuts to God. The market is flooded with surefire, easygoing formulas for a successful life that can be practiced in your spare time. Don't fall for that stuff, even though crowds of people do. The way to life — to God! — is vigorous and requires total attention."

It is sad that so many will be caught up with the crowd and never see the glory of heaven. What is even worse, their destination will be a terrible place to spend eternity. The place is called hell, and I assure you it is as real as heaven is. Jesus spoke more about hell than He did about heaven, and for a good reason. He loves us so much, the last thing He wants to behold is His created humans suffering in such a place.

Many have said that there is not such a place as hell because God, who is supposed to be a God of love, would never place human beings into such eternal torment. Let me clarify something for you. God created hell for Satan and his angels. It was never God's intent that we should go to this place. That decision, my friend, is made by you, not by the God of the Universe. When you make the decision to follow some other god and refuse to believe in Jesus Christ, the Son of the only God, you are making the decision to enter the broad way, which is crowded with millions who are on their way to a terrible place of torment, never to be seen or heard from again.

It is my prayer that no one would enter such damnation. If you haven't asked Jesus into your heart, I invite you to do so right now. Stop reading, get down on your knees, and ask Him to forgive you of your sins and to come into your life today.

Please don't allow the world or some religion to convince you that you are a good person, a person who gives to charities and to the poor and needy, so you have no worries about entering God's heaven. Friend, all of that is not enough. You must confess that you are a sinner, which we all are. You will never kneel to God for forgiveness until you accept the fact that you are a sinner, unclean before a Holy God. Repent today and turn to the Savior who died for your sins on an old, rugged cross. He did it for you and me because He loved us so much.

John 3:16 says, "For God so loved the world that He gave His only begotten Son, that whoever believes in Him should not perish but have everlasting life."

CHAPTER 21

LOVE YOUR NEIGHBOR

But when the Pharisees heard that He had silenced the Sadducees, they gathered together. Then one of them, a lawyer, asked Him a question, testing Him, and saying, "Teacher, which is the great commandment in the law?" Jesus said to him, "'You shall love the Lord your God with all your heart, with all your soul, and with all your mind.' This is the first and great commandment. And the second is like it: 'You shall love your neighbor as yourself.' On these two commandments hang all the Law and the Prophets." (Matthew 22:34-40)

It seems we have become insensitive to the people who share the world with us. We live each day in our own little world with our own cares, never thinking about anyone but ourselves.

Our nation has been divided into so many groups, it is hard to tell one group from another. Lincoln repeated the Scripture when he said, "A house divided cannot stand." I believe that statement stands on solid ground and is certainly good advice for the people of America today.

Our founding fathers probably never thought or considered there would be such divisive behavior in the future of the country they fought so hard to bring freedom and liberty to.

We have fought a great Civil War at a cost of thousands of American lives because of divisions among our leaders. The war put an end to slavery. Slavery was a terrible experience for black people who were sold to the slave traders by their own people in Africa. They were taken from their beloved homeland and scattered across the American continent.

The character of some Americans has left me speechless. I would never have believed the actions of adult people in our country today. Burning down people's businesses and destroying monuments that have stood for years. These folks have no morals and no consideration for others. Killing people regardless of color with no remorse. Attacking police officers and taking their lives, if possible.

Our leaders across the country seem to have lost all common sense. Some are wanting to defund their police departments, saying we don't need police, we need community service-type people. Look at what the Bible says about this:

> Let every soul be subject to the governing authorities. For there is no authority except from God, and the authorities that exist are appointed by God. Therefore whoever resists the authority resists the ordinance of God, and those who resist will bring judgment on themselves. For rulers are not a terror to good works, but to evil. Do you want to be unafraid of the authority? Do what is good, and you will have praise from the same. For he is God's minister to you for good. But if you do evil, be afraid; for he does not bear the sword in vain; for he is God's minister, an avenger to execute wrath on him who practices evil. Therefore you must be subject, not only because of wrath but also for conscience' sake. (Romans 13:1-5)

Remember what I said back in chapter four about discipline, and that not everybody gets a trophy? Read it again and look at what is happening. These are the children with no Bible in the schools and no prayer. We have asked God to leave the country and told our children that God is dead; now we reap the harvest of our sinful ignorance.

The greatest problem in the country today is a heart problem. Without God, the heart is hardened, and people become their own gods. What comes forth from men and women is what is in the heart: "But those things which proceed out of the mouth come from the heart, and they defile a man. For out of the heart proceed evil thoughts, murders, adulteries, fornications, thefts, false witness, blasphemies. These are the things which defile a man" (Matthew 15:18-20).

There is a cure for this heart condition. It is found in the Bible, and the cure is Jesus Christ. When Jesus takes up residence in the heart, the sins listed above are covered by the blood of Jesus Himself. The heart goes through a metamorphosis. The mind steps in line with heart, and the outward actions and words begin to change, just like a butterfly. The person is renewed from the inside out. Romans 12:9-21 describes the results of the change that is made in a person:

Let love be without hypocrisy. Abhor what is evil. Cling to what is good. Be kindly affectionate to one another with brotherly love, in honor giving preference to one another; not lagging in diligence, fervent in spirit, serving the Lord; rejoicing in hope, patient in tribulation, continuing steadfastly in prayer; distributing to the needs of the saints, given to hospitality. Bless those who persecute you; bless and do not curse. Rejoice with those who rejoice, and weep with those who weep. Be of the same mind toward one another. Do not set your mind on high things, but associate with the humble. Do not be wise in your own opinion. Repay no one evil for evil. Have regard for good things in the sight of all men. If it is possible, as much as depends on you, live peaceably with all men. Beloved, do not avenge yourselves, but rather give place to wrath; for it is written, "Vengeance is Mine, I will repay," says the Lord. Therefore "If your enemy is hungry, feed him; If he is thirsty, give him a drink; For in so doing you will heap coals of fire on his head." Do not be overcome by evil, but overcome evil with good.

CHAPTER 22

LOOKING TO THE FUTURE

The future is a part of life we often contemplate, a time we would like to predict, but something that is beyond our control in most cases. Moviemakers and authors have portrayed it in many ways, from future space flight to sleek and aerodynamic automobiles.

I remember in elementary school we signed up for a little magazine. It was called the Weekly Reader. It always contained an article or two about what we could expect in the future. For a little farm boy, it was so exciting to read about space flight and fast cars.

I recollect one article about flying cars. It filled my mind with thoughts of driving out of the driveway and taking off into the magnificent blue sky, flying through the massive white clouds that glide so effortlessly through the sky as they are piloted by the wind, flying to sensational places I have never been, seeing things and places from God's point of view.

Another article about the superhighways of the future would allow vehicles to travel at speeds near a hundred miles per hour. Wow! Imagine how fast we could travel from state to state.

My dad owned a full-service gas station back in the seventies in West Pelzer, a quaint small town. There were several older gentlemen who loved to come and hang out and play checkers at the station. I remember one elderly gentlemen who hated to lose at checkers. One day things were kind of slow, and we were all sitting around watching him play one of the other guys. I was sitting up on the Coca-Cola box, eating peanuts that I'd poured into a six-ounce Coke. I had a bird's eye view of the board and could see that George was slowly losing the game. When he was losing, he had a knack of shaking his collected checkers in his hand, making an annoying sound to distract his opponent. Suddenly George moved into a trap, and as soon as he saw it, he immediately knocked the board off the barrel it was sitting on. Checkers flew all around the room. Everyone began to laugh, because it wasn't the first time George had an accident with board when he knew he was beat. It is amazing how simple times once were.

Conversations would include all sorts of fascinating subjects, from baseball to politics. One day we were informed by the oil company that there was a gas shortage. No one could believe, with all the oil wells in the great state of Texas, that we could possibly be running out of gas. The talk of the day was the shortage, and I told the story about the article in the Weekly Reader about high-speed travel on the superhighways. I said to them, "We have the highways, but we ran out of gas." We all had a good laugh. The lesson learned is the future is unquestionably volatile, and it adjusts without warning, affecting the projected outcome.

There are times when we determine our future by our individual actions or decisions. There are numerous people who made poor decisions because of undesirable behavior early in their lives, which affected their opportunities. For instance, I met a young man who was applying for a position in our organization. He failed to meet the requirements because he broke the law as a teenager. The charge will follow him through life.

I have sat with people who smoked all of their lives only to find out they had lung cancer or heart failure. There are also those who made the decision to take the first drink of alcohol, never realizing the cost of alcoholism.

Every decision we make influences our future. It reminds me of

Abraham in the Old Testament. He was a man who lived in a small town in the ancient Middle East. Just an average person living life with family and friends, not all that concerned about his future. While sitting at home one day, he heard a voice, a voice he did not recognize. The voice was soft but direct. It was the voice of God. Abraham was worshiping false gods, some carved from wood, others hewn from stone. These gods had never spoken audibly to him, much less called him to do something extraordinary. Genesis 12:1-3 records God's words to Abraham:

> *Now the Lord had said to Abram: "Get out of your country, From your family And from your father's house To a land that I will show you. I will make you a great nation; I will bless you And make your name great; And you shall be a blessing. I will bless those who bless you, And I will curse him who curses you; And in you all the families of the earth shall be blessed."*

Can you imagine somebody, especially someone you cannot see — and you certainly have not one indication who they may be or from where they originated — asking you to pull up roots and leave behind all that is dear to you? Quite a request, would you not agree? I think you would concur that this would be unsettling to the typical person.

God called Abraham to be the father of a nation. Abraham responded by following God's request. His choice was a world-changing decision. He never realized his positive response to God would be so valuable.

There is one absolute in the future, and that is judgment. Many live today as if there is no tomorrow, but there are some things that are set in stone. We will die, and there is something beyond the grave. There will be a day for accounting for what we did in this life.

We will never know what the future holds for us, but we know who holds the future.

CPSIA information can be obtained
at www.ICGtesting.com
Printed in the USA
BVHW030615180822
644880BV00005B/30

9 781955 295178